THINK TWICE

Harnessing the Power of Counterintuition

THINK TWICE

MICHAEL J. MAUBOUSSIN

Harvard Business Press

Boston, Massachusetts

Printed in the United States of America

13 12 11 10 09 5 4 3 2

No part of this publication may be reproduced, stored in or introduced into a
retrieval system, or transmitted, in any form, or by any means (electronic, mechanical, photocopying, recording, or otherwise), without the prior permission of the publisher. Requests for permission should be directed to permissions@hbsp.harvard.edu,
or mailed to Permissions, Harvard Business School Publishing, 60 Harvard Way,
Boston, Massachusetts 02163.

Library of Congress Cataloging-in-Publication Data

Mauboussin, Michael J., 1964-
Think twice : harnessing the power of counterintuition / Michael J. Mauboussin.
    p. cm.
Includes bibliographical references.
ISBN 978-1-4221-7675-7 (hbk : alk. paper)
1. Decision making. I. Title.
HD30.23M377 2009
658.4'03–dc22

                                              2009019389

The paper used in this publication meets the requirements of the American National
Standard for Permanence of Paper for Publications and Documents in Libraries and
Archives Z39.48-1992.

To Al Rappaport

Mentor, collaborator, friend

CONTENTS

ACKNOWLEDGMENTS

I am deeply grateful to be in the position to learn from thoughtful and wonderful people. The individuals who encouraged, guided, and taught me in the process of writing *Think Twice* made the long journey rich and fulfilling.

My colleagues at Legg Mason Capital Management have been terrific, providing valuable support and cooperation. That I was able to write this book during a difficult time in the markets is a testament to the organization's commitment to learning. In particular, Bill Miller and Kyle Legg provided me with the needed flexibility to take on this challenge, and I hope that I can repay their confidence in full.

A number of people graciously shared their time and knowledge with me. They told me stories, clarified points, or aimed me in the right direction when I was off track. These include Orley Ashenfelter, Greg Berns, Angela Freymuth Caveney, Clayton Christensen, Katrina Firlik, Brian Roberson, Phil Rosenzweig, Jeff Severts, Thomas Thurston, and Duncan Watts.

Getting ideas right is not always easy. I was privileged to have a small group, each a leader in his field, read and critique sections of the book. My thanks to Steven Crist, Scott Page, Tom Seeley, Stephen Stigler, Steve Strogatz, and David Weinberger.

The Santa Fe Institute has been a tremendous source of learning and inspiration for me. SFI takes a multidisciplinary approach to understanding the common themes that arise in complex systems. The institute attracts people who are intellectually curious and collaborative, and I am appreciative of the willingness of the scientists, staff, and network members to share so much with me. Particular thanks go to Doug Erwin, Shannon Larsen, John Miller, Scott Page, and Geoffrey West.

Reading a draft of a manuscript and providing feedback to the author is difficult and time-consuming. I was fortunate to have a stellar collection of folks, from many walks of life, help me out. These include Paul DePodesta, Doug Erwin, Dick Foster, Michelle Mauboussin, Bill Miller, Michael Persky, Al Rappaport, David Shaywitz, and three anonymous reviewers. Thanks to all of you for your valuable time and very helpful recommendations.

I have long been an admirer of Daniel Kahneman's work. But in doing the research for this book, my respect for his contributions to psychology in general and to decision making in particular grew immensely. He is deservedly a towering figure in psychology, and his work touched almost every idea in this book.

I want to offer special recognition to my friend Laurence Gonzales. Over the years, Laurence and I have asked many of the same questions about decision making. But because he has a very different background and set of experiences than me, he has opened my eyes to many new and useful points of view. Just his willingness to share his thoughts with me has put me in his debt.

But Laurence, a very talented writer, went well beyond swapping ideas with me. Upon receiving a draft of the book, he made the extraordinary offer to edit it in full. Working through his comments was some of the hardest and most rewarding work I have ever done. He taught me about the craft of writing, compelled me to sharpen my thinking, and insisted on clarity. With Laurence, the writing serves the ideas and not the other way around. I cannot thank you enough, Laurence.

Dan Callahan, a colleague at Legg Mason Capital Management, was integral to the project. Dan provided essential research support and coordinated the exhibits. Most importantly, he read numerous drafts of the chapters and provided useful feedback. He also did much of this while juggling other responsibilities, going above and beyond the call of duty. Dan, a big thanks to you.

I would also like to acknowledge A. J. Alper, who thought of the title (including the "thin ice" angle) and graciously allowed me to use it. A. J. is a pleasure to work with and has a great balance between creativity and business sense.

I'd like to thank Kirsten Sandberg, my editor at Harvard Business Press, for shepherding this project from a brainstorming session to a final product. Volleying ideas with Kirsten is always beneficial, and her feedback sharpened the manuscript in important ways. I appreciate Kirsten for never letting me lose sight of our audience, our message, and how to connect the two. Ania Wieckowski was also great throughout the editorial process in matters big and small, and Jen Waring made the production smooth and efficient.

My wife, Michelle, is a constant source of love, support, and counsel. She also encourages me, and allows me, to pursue my passions. Michelle's comments about the initial manuscript were direct and on point in a way that only a wife could pull off. My mother, Clotilde Mauboussin, has been a steadfast force in my life and provided me with all of the opportunities I could have asked for. My mother-in-law, Andrea Maloney Schara, is part our family's day-to-day life and maintains an admirable thirst for learning. Finally, I thank my children Andrew, Alex, Madeline, Isabelle, and Patrick. Each of them helped me to write this book in some way, and I hope that they will find the ideas useful in their lives some day.

Smart Is as Smart Does

IN DECEMBER 2008, two seemingly unrelated events occurred. The first was the release of Stephen Greenspan's book, *Annals of Gullibility: Why We Get Duped and How to Avoid It*. Greenspan, a professor of psychology, explained why we allow other people to take advantage of us and discussed gullibility in fields including finance, academia, and the law. He ended the book with helpful advice on becoming less gullible.

The second was the exposure of the greatest Ponzi scheme in history, run by Bernard Madoff, which cost its unsuspecting investors in excess of $60 billion. A Ponzi scheme is a fraudulent operation in which a manager uses funds from new investors to pay off old investors. Since there is no legitimate investment activity, it collapses when the operator can't find enough additional investors. Madoff's scheme unraveled when he couldn't meet requests for redemptions from the investors stung by the financial meltdown.

The irony is that Greenspan, who is bright and well regarded, lost 30 percent of his retirement savings in Madoff's Ponzi scheme.[1] The guy who wrote the book on gullibility got taken by one of the greatest scammers of all time. In fairness, Greenspan didn't know Madoff. He invested in a fund that turned the money over to the scheme. And Greenspan has been gracious in sharing his story and explaining why he was drawn to investment returns that looked, in retrospect, too good to be true.

If you ask people to offer adjectives they associate with good decision makers, words like "intelligent" and "smart" are generally at the top of the list. But history contains plenty of examples of intelligent people who made poor decisions, with horrific consequences, as the result of cognitive mistakes. Consider the following:

- In the summer of 1998, Long-Term Capital Management (LTCM), a U.S. hedge fund, lost over $4 billion and had to be bailed out by a consortium of banks. The senior professionals at LTCM, who included two recipients of the Nobel Prize in economics, were highly successful up to that point. As a group, the professionals were among the most intellectually impressive of any organization in the world and were large investors in their own fund. They failed because their financial models didn't sufficiently consider large asset price fluctuations.[2]

- On February 1, 2003, the U.S. space shuttle *Columbia* disintegrated when reentering the Earth's atmosphere, killing all seven crew members. The engineers at the National Aeronautics and Space Administration (NASA) were considered the best and the brightest in the world. *Columbia* broke up because a piece of foam insulation broke off during the launch and damaged the shuttle's ability to protect itself from heat on reentry. The problem of foam debris was not new, but since nothing bad had happened in the past, the engineers overlooked the issue. Rather than considering the risks from the debris, NASA took the lack of problems as evidence that everything was okay.[3]

- Within a few weeks in the fall of 2008, Iceland's three largest banks collapsed, its currency dropped by more than 70 percent, and its stock market lost more than 80 percent of its value. After the banking sector was privatized in 2003, the large banks increased their assets from roughly one times Iceland's GDP to close to ten times GDP, "the most rapid expansion of a banking system in the history of mankind." Known as a country of well-educated and measured people, Iceland's citizens went on a debt-fueled spending spree, driving up asset prices. While each person might be able to rationalize his own decisions, collectively the country ran off an economic cliff.[4]

No one wakes up thinking, "I am going to make bad decisions today." Yet we all make them. What is particularly surprising is some of the biggest mistakes are made by people who are, by objective standards, very intelligent. Smart people make big, dumb, and consequential mistakes.

Keith Stanovich, a psychologist at the University of Toronto, argues that the intelligence quotient (IQ) tests we rely on to judge who is smart do not measure the essential raw materials for making quality decisions. "Although most people would say that the ability to think rationally is a clear sign of superior intellect," he writes, "standard IQ tests devote no section to rational thinking."[5] Mental flexibility, introspection, and the ability to properly calibrate evidence are at the core of rational thinking and are largely absent on IQ tests.

Smart people make poor decisions because they have the same factory settings on their mental software as the rest of us, and that software isn't designed to cope with many of today's problems. So our minds frequently want to see the world one way—the default—while a better way to see the world takes some mental effort. A simple example is an optical illusion: you perceive one image while the reality is something different.

Beyond the problem of mental software, smart people also make bad decisions because they harbor false beliefs. For instance, Sir Arthur Conan Doyle, known best as the creator of the detective Sherlock Holmes, believed in many forms of spiritualism, such as the existence of fairies. These beliefs prevent clear thinking. To make good decisions, you frequently must think twice—and that's something our minds would rather not do.

This focus on mistakes may sound depressing, but this book is really a story of opportunity. The opportunity comes in two flavors. You can reduce the number of mistakes you make by thinking about problems more clearly. According to research by Stanovich and others, if you explain to intelligent people how they might go wrong with a problem before they decide, they do much better than if they solve the problem with no guidance. "Intelligent people perform better only when you tell them what to do!" exclaims Stanovich. Also, you can see and capitalize on the mistakes that other people make. As shrewd businesspeople know, one man's mistake is another's opportunity. Over time, the most rational thinker will win. *Think Twice* is about identifying these opportunities.

I will take you through three steps:

- *Prepare.* The first step is mental preparation, which requires you to learn about the mistakes. In each chapter, I discuss a mistake, with examples from a range of professions, and use academic research to explain why you make them. I also examine how these mistakes have big consequences. Even though they have the best of intentions, investors, businesspeople, doctors, lawyers, government officials, and other professionals routinely botch their decisions, often with extremely high costs.

- *Recognize.* Once you are aware of the categories of mistakes, the second step is to recognize the problems in context, or situational awareness. Here, your goal is to recognize the kind of problem you face, how you risk making a mistake, and which tools you need to choose wisely. Mistakes generally arise from the mismatch between the complex reality you face and the simplifying mental routines you use to cope with that complexity. The challenge is to make intellectual links between realms that may not appear similar on the surface. As you will see, a multidisciplinary approach can yield great insight into decision making.

- *Apply.* The third and most important step is to mitigate your potential mistakes. The goal is to build or refine a set of mental tools to cope with the realities of life, much as an athlete develops a repertoire of skills to prepare for a game. Many of these tips involve keeping your intuition in check while using an approach that feels counterintuitive.

By the way, I claim no immunity from these cognitive mistakes and still fall for every one that I describe in the book. My personal goal is to recognize when I enter a danger zone while trying to make a decision and to slow down when I do. Finding the proper point of view at the appropriate time is critical.

Prepare, Recognize, Apply—and Win a T-Shirt

Like many instructors of finance, I do experiments with my students to show how bright people fall into traps while making decisions. In one experiment, I present the class with a jar of coins and ask everyone to bid independently on the value of its contents. Most students bid below the actual value, but some bid well above the coins' worth. The highest bidder wins the auction but overpays for the coins. This is known as "the winner's curse." It's important in corporate mergers and acquisitions, because when companies bid against one another to buy a target corporation, the highest bidder frequently pays too much. The experiment gives the students (doubly so the winner) firsthand experience.[6]

To spice up such experiments, instructors often turn them into contests with prizes for the individuals who do best. I attended a two-day conference on "Investment Decisions and Behavioral Finance" at Harvard University that included a couple of those contests. My reading and teaching had familiarized me with these experiments. When I first tried them, I did poorly—below average. But I then studied the principles, practiced identifying the problems, and learned the techniques to approach them properly.

The first was a test of overconfidence. Richard Zeckhauser, a political scientist at Harvard University and a champion bridge player, gave each participant a list of ten unusual questions of fact (e.g., gestation period of an Asian elephant) and asked for both a best guess and a high and low estimate, bounding the correct answer with 90 percent confidence. For example, I might reason that an elephant's gestation is longer than a human's and guess fifteen months. I might also feel 90 percent assured that the answer is somewhere between twelve and eighteen months. If my ability matches my confidence, then I would expect the correct answers to fall within that range nine times out of ten. But, in fact, most people are correct only 40 to 60 percent of the time, reflecting their overconfidence.[7] Even though I didn't know the answers to those ten questions, I had a sense of where I might go wrong, so I adjusted my initial estimates. I won that contest and got a book.

The second experiment showed the failure of pure rationality. Here, Richard Thaler, one of the world's foremost behavioral economists, asked us to write down a whole number from zero to one hundred, with the prize going to the person whose guess was closest to two-thirds of the group's average guess. In a purely rational world, all participants would coolly carry out as many levels of deduction as necessary to get to the experiment's logical solution—zero. But the game's real challenge involves considering the behavior of the other participants. You may score intellectual points by going with naught, but if anyone selects a number greater than zero, you win no prize. The winning answer, incidentally, is generally between eleven and thirteen.[8] I won that contest too, and got a T-shirt.

As Thaler tossed me my prize, he grumbled, "You don't deserve this because you knew what was going on."

Yes, I did know what was going on. *That was the point.* And that is the point of this book.

The Magic Square: Making Hard Problems Easy

Preparation and recognition give you new points of view that can make tough problems simpler. One example is a game called Sum-to-Fifteen, conceived by the celebrated economist, Herbert Simon.

You lay nine cards, numbered one through nine, face up on a table. Two players alternate selecting cards with the goal of collecting three cards that add up to fifteen. If you've never played the game before, try it. Or offer to try it on some friends or colleagues and watch carefully as they go back and forth.

The game is moderately hard, because you must keep in your head a running total of your numbers as well as those of your opponent. You must think offensively, getting three cards that add up to fifteen, as well as defensively, preventing your opponent from doing the same. It is common for one person to win as his opponent gets tangled in the numbers.

Now I'll introduce a magic square that makes the game much easier:

$$8 \quad 3 \quad 4$$
$$1 \quad 5 \quad 9$$
$$6 \quad 7 \quad 2$$

Note the numbers sum to fifteen if you look at them vertically, horizontally, or diagonally. All of a sudden, the game becomes very easy: it's the childhood favorite, tic-tac-toe (also known as naughts and crosses). Once you perceive the game as tic-tac-toe, the winning path is much clearer. A tie should be a worst-case scenario, and losing is, well, inexcusable.[9]

Most people do not find it natural to match ideas from their mental database to tricky situations in the real world. Our brains are not wired for the process of moving from preparation to recognition. Indeed, typical decision makers allocate only 25 percent of their time to thinking about the problem properly and learning from experience. Most spend their time gathering information, which feels like progress and appears diligent to superiors. But information without context is falsely empowering. If you do not properly understand the challenges involved in your decision, this data will offer nothing to improve the accuracy of the decision and actually may create misplaced confidence.[10]

Process or Outcome: Which Should You Focus On?

Three factors determine the outcomes of your decisions: how you think about the problem, your actions, and luck. You can familiarize yourself with common mistakes, recognize the situation you're in, and take what appears to be the correct action. But luck, by definition, is beyond your control, even though it may determine the outcome (especially over the short term). That statistical reality begs a fundamental question: should you evaluate the quality of your decisions based on the process by which you make the decision or by its outcome?

The intuitive answer is to focus on outcomes. Outcomes are objective and sort winners from losers. In many cases, those evaluating the decision believe that a favorable outcome is *evidence* of a good process. While pervasive, this mode of thinking is a really bad habit. Kicking the habit opens up a world of insight into decision making.

Our most challenging decisions include an element of uncertainty, and at best we can express the possible outcomes as probabilities. Further, we must make decisions even when the information is incomplete. When a decision involves probability, good decisions can lead to bad outcomes, and bad decisions can lead to good outcomes (at least for awhile). Say, for example, that you are playing blackjack in a casino and are dealt cards that add up to eighteen. Going against standard blackjack strategy, you ask for a hit and the dealer flips a three, making your hand. That's a poor process and a favorable outcome. Play that same hand a hundred times, and you will lose on average, as standard strategy acknowledges.

In a probabilistic environment, you are better served by focusing on the process by which you make a decision than on the outcome. Blackjack is a game of chance. That means you will do best by following a rule that reflects the real probability of being dealt the right cards: don't hit when you've been dealt a seventeen or more. But it's crucial to bear in mind that because of the substantial role that luck plays in this process, good decisions don't ensure attractive outcomes. If you make a good decision and suffer a poor outcome, pick yourself up, dust yourself off, and get ready to do it again.

When evaluating other people's decisions, you are again better served by looking at their decision-making process rather than on the outcome. There are plenty of people who succeed largely by chance. More often than not, they are completely unaware of how they did it. But they almost always get their comeuppance when fortune stops smiling on them. Likewise, skillful people who have suffered a period of poor outcomes are often a good bet, since luck evens out over time.[11]

Picking the Main Mistakes We Professionals Make

The primary audience for this book is investors and businesspeople, although the concepts are relevant for other professionals as well. This book is neither a survey of common mistakes nor an exposition of one big theme. For instance, most books focus either on the components of prospect theory (loss aversion, overconfidence, framing effects, anchoring, and the confirmation bias) or they dwell on one important idea.[12] Rather, I have tried to select the concepts that I have found most useful, based on my experience in the investment industry and through my study of psychology and science.

Each of the following chapters discusses a common decision mistake, illustrates why that mistake is consequential, and offers some thoughts on how to manage the problem. Specifically:

- Chapter 1, "The Outside View: Why Big Brown Was a Bad Bet," describes our tendency to consider each problem as unique rather than considering carefully the experience of others. This mistake helps explain why executives express near-universal optimism when acquiring other companies, despite the poor record of acquisition success.

- Chapter 2, "Open to Options: How Your Telephone Number Can Influence Your Decisions," deals with tunnel vision, the failure to consider alternatives under certain conditions. Our minds want to reduce the options at times when we should keep our alternatives open. Also, incentives may encourage certain choices that are good for one person but not another.

- Chapter 3, "The Expert Squeeze: Why Netflix Knows More Than Clerks Do About Your Favorite Films," highlights our uncritical reliance on experts. Experts tend to know about very narrow fields, justifying a skeptical view of the claims and predictions they make. Increasingly, people can more effectively solve problems by making models of decisions using computers or by accessing the wisdom of crowds than by relying on experts.

- Chapter 4, "Situational Awareness: How Accordion Music Boosts Sales of Burgundy," underscores the crucial role of context in decision making. As much as we like to think of ourselves as objective, the behavior of those around us exerts extraordinary influence on our decisions. It also shows why we should not be too quick to judge the behavior of others without fully appreciating the context of their decisions.

- Chapter 5, "More Is Different: How Bees Find the Best Hive Without a Real Estate Agent," explores the pitfalls of understanding complex systems on the wrong level. Attempting to understand macro behavior by aggregating micro behavior fails because the total is greater than the sum of the parts. You can't understand an ant colony by watching what one ant does. The chapter also shows that it is nearly impossible to manage a complex system, a lesson the U.S. government learned as it coped with the financial crisis of 2007–2009.

- Chapter 6, "Evidence of Circumstance: How Outsourcing the Dreamliner Became Boeing's Nightmare," cautions against predicting cause and effect for a system based on attributes rather than circumstances. The answer to most questions in life is, "It depends." This chapter explores how to think about what it depends on.

- Chapter 7, "Grand Ah-Whooms: How Ten Brits Made the Millennium Bridge Wobble," covers phase transitions, in which small perturbations to a system can lead to large changes. Since cause and effect are difficult to identify when phase transitions occur, it's almost impossible to predict the outcome. That's why no one knows where the next hit movie or song will come from.

- Chapter 8, "Sorting Luck from Skill: Why Investors Excel at Buying High and Selling Low," deals with the role of skill and luck in outcomes and emphasizes the concept of reversion to the mean, which is often misunderstood. For example, sports reporters and business commentators are generally oblivious to roles of skill and luck as they report on successes and failures.

- The conclusion, "Time to Think Twice," summarizes advice on how to think about the mistakes discussed throughout the book. It also recommends some specific techniques for gaining a decision-making edge, such as maintaining a decision journal, to put these ideas into practice.

Daniel Kahneman, a psychologist at Princeton University who won the 2002 Nobel Prize in economics, once noted his surprise at how ambivalent people are about the process of decision making.[13] While they talk about improving, very few are willing to spend the time and money necessary to learn and, ultimately, to change. In the following chapters, I will introduce concepts that can help you make better decisions. I hope you will also have some fun along the way.

I chose the themes for each chapter with three criteria in mind. The issues had to be common. Once you internalize a few of these concepts, you will see them everywhere—in the decisions you face as well as in the decisions of others. The concepts had to be identifiable. The themes here are not meant to be subtle or nuanced, and you will see them pop up in places where you may have overlooked them before. Finally, the mistakes associated with the themes had to be preventable. While I can't guarantee you success, I can help you improve how you make decisions.

THINK TWICE

CHAPTER ONE

The Outside View

Why Big Brown Was a Bad Bet

"It's A FOREGONE CONCLUSION." So proclaimed Rick Dutrow on the likelihood that his race horse, Big Brown, would capture the coveted Triple Crown in 2008. Winning the Triple Crown is a tremendous feat. A horse must win the Kentucky Derby, the Preakness Stakes, and the Belmont Stakes on three tracks of different lengths over just five weeks. Before Big Brown's attempt, only eleven horses had succeeded in the preceding century, and none had done so in the previous thirty years. Here was Big Brown, only one race away from horse-racing "immortality."[1]

Dutrow, the horse's trainer, had reason to be optimistic. Not only was his three-year-old colt undefeated in his first five starts, he was dominant. Although the odds makers placed only a 25 percent probability on his winning the Kentucky Derby, Big Brown won by four-and-three-quarters lengths. He was stronger still in the Preakness, crossing the finish line five-and-one-quarter lengths ahead of the field, even though his jockey eased him coming down the home stretch. In his last race, the Belmont, Big Brown faced mediocre competition, and his biggest challenger, Casino Drive, dropped out of the race at the last minute.

Not surprisingly, enthusiasm for Big Brown built. Sensing opportunity, UPS, the company after which Big Brown was named, signed a marketing deal that included a corporate logo on the jacket of Big Brown's outrider. A majority of racetrack pros picked him to win the race. And then there was Big Brown himself. He was portrayed as strong, confident, and ready. Dutrow gushed, "He looks as good as he can possibly look. I can't find any flaws whatsoever in Big Brown. I see the prettiest picture. I'm so confident, it's unbelievable."[2] The fans agreed: attendance for the pivotal race was double what it had been in the previous year despite the sweltering heat, as the crowd yearned to see history made.

Big Brown made history, all right. It just wasn't the kind of history everyone expected. He finished dead last, which no Triple Crown contender had ever done.[3]

Veterinarians gave Big Brown a full physical exam following the race and he appeared to be fine. His capricious performance evoked what lab researchers call Harvard's Law, "Under the most rigorously controlled conditions of pressure, temperature, volume, humidity, and other variables, the organism will do as it damn well pleases."[4]

However, there was another way of looking at Big Brown's chances of winning the Triple Crown, one that was far less optimistic about his prospects of joining the pantheon of horse racing. This point of view asked a simple question: how successful were other horses when they were in Big Brown's position?

Steven Crist, a talented writer and renowned handicapper, provided some sobering statistics.[5] Of the twenty-nine horses with a chance to capture the Triple Crown after winning the Kentucky Derby and the Preakness Stakes, only eleven triumphed, a success rate less than 40 percent. But a closer examination of those statistics yielded a stark difference before and after 1950. Before 1950, eight of the nine horses attempting to win the Triple Crown succeeded. After 1950, only three of twenty horses won. It's hard to know why the achievement rate dropped from nearly 90 percent to just 15 percent, but logical factors include better breeding (leading to more quality foals) and bigger starting fields.

While a 15 percent rate of success may raise some concern, it doesn't take into consideration Big Brown's innate ability and impressive track record. After all, not all of the horses in a position to win the Triple Crown had similar talent. One way to compare horses is the Beyer Speed Figure, which assigns a number to a horse's performance based on the time of the race and the speed of the track, given the weather conditions. Higher speed figures are better.

Table 1-1 shows the speed figures in the first two Triple Crown races for the last seven aspirants, including Big Brown. The sample is small because speed figures have been widely available only since 1991. While his jockey's actions likely pared a few points from his Preakness figure, Big Brown looked downright lead-hoofed when compared to the other horses. Even considering the so-so Belmont field, it was obvious that Big Brown was not certain to win. Yet the bettors had Big Brown's odds at a euphoric three-to-ten, implying he had more than a 75 percent probability of winning the final leg. Crist and other sharp handicappers had the horse sense to recognize the tote board substantially overstated Big Brown's chance of winning.

These contrasting points of view reveal our first mistake, a tendency to favor the inside view over the outside view.[6] An inside view considers a problem by focusing on the specific task and by using information that is close at hand, and makes predictions based on

TABLE 1-1

Beyer Speed Figures for Triple Crown contenders

Horse	Kentucky Derby	Preakness	Total
Silver Charm	115	118	233
Smarty Jones	107	118	225
Funny Cide	109	114	223
War Emblem	114	109	223
Real Quiet	107	111	218
Charismatic	108	107	215
Big Brown	109	100	209

Source: Steven Crist.

that narrow and unique set of inputs. These inputs may include anecdotal evidence and fallacious perceptions. This is the approach that most people use in building models of the future and is indeed common for all forms of planning. Rick Dutrow and the other fans of Big Brown dwelled largely on the inside view, including the horse's wins and imposing physical appearance. This comes naturally but almost always paints too optimistic a picture.

The outside view asks if there are similar situations that can provide a statistical basis for making a decision. Rather than seeing a problem as unique, the outside view wants to know if others have faced comparable problems and, if so, what happened. The outside view is an unnatural way to think, precisely because it forces people to set aside all the cherished information they have gathered. Handicappers using the outside view judged Big Brown to be a very poor bet, as the experience of other horses in the same spot suggested a probability of winning that was much lower than what was on the tote board. The outside view can often create a very valuable reality check for decision makers.

Why do people tend to embrace the inside view? Most of us are unduly optimistic a good deal of the time. Social psychologists distinguish three illusions that lead people to the inside view.[7]

To introduce the first illusion, take a moment to answer (honestly!) the following questions either yes or no:

- I am an above-average driver.

- I have an above-average ability to judge humor.

- My professional performance places me in the top half of my organization.

If you are like most people, you said yes to all three questions. This shows the illusion of superiority, which suggests people have an unrealistically positive view of themselves. Of course, not everyone can be above average. In a classic 1976 survey, the College Board asked high school test takers to rate themselves on a host of criteria. Eighty-five percent considered themselves above the median in getting along with others, 70 percent above the median in ability to lead others, and 60 percent above the median in sports. One survey showed that more than 80 percent of people believed that they were more skillful than half of all drivers.[8]

Remarkably, the least capable people often have the largest gaps between what they think they can do and what they actually achieve.[9] In one study, researchers asked subjects to rate their perceived ability and likely success on a grammar test. Figure 1-1 shows that the poorest performers dramatically overstated their ability, thinking that they would be in the next-to-highest quartile. They turned in results in the bottom quartile. Furthermore, even when individuals do acknowledge that they are below average, they tend to dismiss their shortcomings as inconsequential.

FIGURE 1-1

The least competent are often the most confident

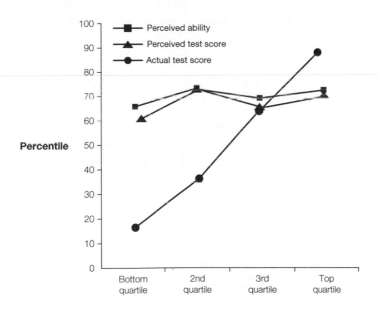

Source: Justin Kruger and David Dunning, "Unskilled and Unaware of It: How Difficulties in Recognizing One's Own Incompetence Lead to Inflated Self-Assessments." *Journal of Personality and Social Psychology* 77, no. 6 (1999): 1121–1134.

The second is the illusion of optimism. Most people see their future as brighter than that of others. For example, researchers asked college students to estimate their chances of having various good and bad experiences during their lives. The students judged themselves far more likely to have good experiences than their peers, and far less likely to have bad experiences.[10]

Finally, there is the illusion of control. People behave as if chance events are subject to their control. For instance, people rolling dice throw softly when they want to roll low numbers and hard for high numbers. In one study, researchers asked two groups of office workers to participate in a lottery, with a $1 cost and a $50 prize. One group was allowed to choose their lottery cards, while the other group had no choice. Luck determined the probability of winning, of course, but that's not how the workers behaved.

Before the drawing, one of the researchers asked the participants at what price they would be willing to sell their cards. The mean offer for the group that was allowed to choose cards was close to $9, while the offer from the group that had not chosen was less than $2. People who believe that they have some control have the perception that their odds of success are better than they actually are. People who don't have a sense of control don't experience the same bias.[11]

I must concede that my occupation, active money management, may be one of the best examples of the illusion of control in the professional world. Researchers have shown that, in aggregate, money managers who actively build portfolios deliver returns lower than the market indexes over time, a finding that every investment firm acknowledges.[12] The reason is pretty straightforward: markets are highly competitive, and money managers charge fees that diminish returns. Markets also have a good dose of randomness, assuring that all investors see good and poor results from time to time. Despite the evidence, active money managers behave as if they can defy the odds and deliver market-beating returns. These investment firms rely on the inside view to justify their strategies and fees.

The Odds of Success Are Poor . . . But Not for Me

A vast range of professionals commonly lean on the inside view to make important decisions with predictably poor results. This is not to say these decision makers are negligent, naïve, or malicious. Encouraged by the three illusions, most believe they are making the right decision and have faith that the outcomes will be satisfactory. Now that you are aware of the distinction between the inside and outside view, you can measure your decisions and the decisions of others more carefully. Let's look at some examples.

Corporate mergers and acquisitions (M&A) are a multitrillion dollar global business year in and year out. Corporations spend vast sums identifying, acquiring, and integrating companies in order gain a strategic edge. There is little doubt that companies make deals with the best of intentions.

The problem is that most deals don't create value for the shareholders of the acquiring company (shareholders of the companies that are bought do fine, on average). In fact, researchers estimate that when one company buys another, the acquiring company's stock goes down roughly two-thirds of the time.[13] Given that most managers have an explicit objective of increasing value—and that their compensation is often tied to the stock price—the vigor of the M&A market appears moderately surprising. The explanation is that while most executives recognize that the overall M&A record is not good, they believe that they can beat the odds.

"A high-quality beachfront property" is how the chief executive officer of Dow Chemical described Rohm and Haas after Dow agreed to acquire the company in July 2008. Dow was undaunted by the bidding war, which had driven the price premium it had to pay to a steep 74 percent. Instead, the CEO declared the deal "a decisive step towards establishing Dow as an earnings-growth company."[14] The enthusiasm of Dow's management had all the hallmarks of the inside view. When the deal was announced, the stock price of Dow Chemical slumped

4 percent, putting the deal on top of a growing pile of losses suffered through acquisitions.

Basic math explains why most companies don't add value when they acquire another firm. The change in value for the buyer equals the difference between the increase in cash flow from combining the two companies (synergies) and the amount over the market value that the acquirer pays (premium). Companies want to get more than they pay for. So if synergies exceed the premium, the price of the buyer's stock will rise. If not, it will fall. In this case, the value of the synergy—based on Dow's own figures—was less than the premium it paid, justifying a drop in price. Glowing rhetoric aside, the numbers were not good for the shareholders of Dow Chemical.[15]

The Plural of Anecdote Is Not Evidence

A few years ago, my father was diagnosed with late-stage cancer. After the chemotherapy failed, he was basically out of options. One day, he called seeking my advice. He had read a magazine advertisement about an alternative cancer treatment that claimed near-miraculous results and pointed to a Web site full of glowing testimonials. If he sent me the information, would I tell him what I thought?

It didn't take long to do the research. No well-constructed studies had shown the treatment's efficacy, and the evidence in favor of the approach amounted to a collection of anecdotes. When my father called back, I could hear in his voice that his mind was made up. Despite the substantial cost and taxing travel, he wanted to pursue this long-shot alternative. When he asked me what I thought, I told him, "I try to think like a scientist. And based on everything I can see, this won't work." Hanging up the phone, I felt torn. I wanted to believe the story and go with the inside view. I wanted my father to be well again. But the scientist in me admonished me to stick with the outside view. Even considering the power of the placebo effect, hope is not a strategy.

My father died shortly after that episode, but the experience compelled me to think about how we decide about our medical treatments.

For a long time, the paternalistic model reigned in relationships between physicians and patients. Physicians would diagnose a condition and select the treatment that seemed best for the patient. Patients nowadays are more informed and generally want to take part in making decisions. Physicians and patients frequently discuss the pros and cons of various treatments and together select the best course of action. Indeed, studies show that patients involved in making those decisions are more satisfied with their medical treatment.

But research also suggests that patients regularly make choices that are not in their best interests, often due to a failure to consider the outside view.[16] In one study, researchers presented subjects with a fictitious disease and various treatments. Each subject had a choice between two treatments. The first, the control treatment, had 50 percent effectiveness. The second was one of twelve options that combined a positive, neutral, or negative anecdote about a fictional patient with four possible levels of effectiveness, ranging from 30 percent to 90 percent.

The stories made a huge difference and swamped the base-rate data in the decision-making process. Table 1-2 tells the tale. Patients selected a treatment with 90 percent effectiveness less than 40 percent of the time when it was paired with a story about a failed

TABLE 1-2

Are anecdotes more important than antidotes?

Percent of subjects choosing the treatment

| | BASE RATE | | | |
	90%	70%	50%	30%
Positive anecdote	88	92	93	78
Neutral anecdote	81	81	69	29
Negative anecdote	39	43	15	7

Source: Angela K. Freymuth and George F. Ronan, "Modeling Patient Decision-Making: The Role of Base-Rate and Anecdotal Information," *Journal of Clinical Psychology in Medical Settings* 11, no. 3 (2004): 211–216.

patient. Conversely, nearly 80 percent of the patients selected a treatment with 30 percent effectiveness when it was matched with a success story. The results of this study were fully consistent with my father's behavior.

While it's good for patients to be informed and engaged, they run the risk of being influenced by sources that rely predominantly on anecdotes, including friends, family, the Internet, and mass media. Doctors might find anecdotes to be an effective way of getting their points across to patients. But doctors and patients should be careful not to lose sight of the scientific evidence.[17]

On Time and Within Budget—Maybe Next Time

You will be familiar with this example if you have ever been part of a project, whether it involved renovating a house, introducing a new product, or meeting a work deadline. People find it hard to estimate how long a job will take and how much it will cost. When they are wrong, they usually underestimate the time and expense. Psychologists call this the planning fallacy. Here again, the inside view takes over, as the majority of people imagine how they will complete the task. Only about one-quarter of the population incorporates the base-rate data either from their own experience or from that of others, while laying out planning timetables.

Roger Buehler, a professor of psychology at Wilfrid Laurier University, did an experiment that illustrates the point. Buehler and his collaborators asked college students how long it would take to complete a school assignment with three levels of chance: 50, 75, and 99 percent. For example, a subject might say that there was a 50 percent chance that he would finish the project by next Monday, a 75 percent chance he'd be done by Wednesday, and a 99 percent chance by Friday.

Figure 1-2 shows how accurate the estimates were: when the deadline arrived for which the students had given themselves a 50 percent chance of finishing, only 13 percent actually turned in their work. At the point when the students thought there was 75 percent chance they'd be done, just 19 percent had completed the project. All the students were virtually sure they'd be done by the final date. But only 45 percent turned out to be right. As Buehler and his fellow researchers note, "Even when asked to make a highly conservative forecast, a prediction that they felt virtually certain that they would fulfill, students' confidence in their time estimates far exceeded their accomplishments."[18]

This work has an interesting twist. While people are notoriously poor at guessing when they'll finish their own projects, they're pretty good at guessing about other people. In fact, the planning fallacy embodies a broader principle. When people are forced to look at similar situations and see the frequency of success, they tend to predict more accurately. If you want to know how something

FIGURE 1-2

There's a huge gap between when people believe they will complete a task and when they actually do

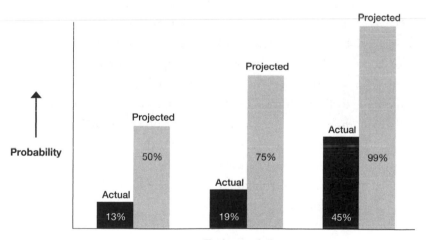

Source: Roger Buehler, Dale Griffin, and Michael Ross, "It's About Time: Optimistic Predictions in Work and Love," in *European Review of Social Psychology*, vol. 6, ed. Wolfgang Stroebe and Miles Hewstone (Chichester, UK: John Wiley & Sons, 1995), 1–32.

is going to turn out for you, look at how it turned out for others in the same situation. Daniel Gilbert, a psychologist at Harvard University, ponders why people don't rely more on the outside view, "Given the impressive power of this simple technique, we should expect people to go out of their way to use it. But they don't." The reason is most people think of themselves as different, and better, than those around them.[19]

Now that you are aware of how the inside-outside view influences the way people make decisions, you'll see it everywhere. In the business world, it will show up as unwarranted optimism for how long it takes to develop a new product, the chance that a merger deal succeeds, and the likelihood a portfolio of stocks will do better than the market. In your personal life, you'll see it in the parents who believe their seven-year-old is destined for a college sports scholarship, debates about what impact video games have on kids, and the time and cost it will take to remodel a kitchen.

Even people who should know better forget to consult the outside view. Years ago, Daniel Kahneman assembled a group to write a curriculum to teach judgment and decision making to high school students. Kahneman's group included a mix of experienced and inexperienced teachers as well as the dean of the school of education. After about a year, they had written a couple of chapters for the textbook and had developed some sample lessons.

During one of their Friday afternoon sessions, the educators discussed how to elicit information from groups and how to think about the future. They knew that the best way to do this was for each person to express his or her view independently and to combine the views into a consensus. Kahneman decided to make the exercise tangible by asking each member to estimate the date the group would deliver a draft of the textbook to the Ministry of Education.

Kahneman found that the estimates clustered around two years and that everyone, including the dean, estimated between eighteen and thirty months. It then occurred to Kahneman that the dean had been involved in similar projects. When asked, the dean said he knew of a number of similar groups, including ones that had worked on the biology and mathematics curriculum. So Kahneman asked him the obvious question: "How long did it take them to finish?"

The dean blushed and then answered that 40 percent of the groups that had started similar programs had never finished, and that none of the groups completed it in less than seven years. Seeing only one way to reconcile the dean's optimistic answer about this group with his knowledge of the shortcomings of the other groups, Kahneman asked how good this group was compared with the others. After a pause, the dean responded, "Below average, but not by much."[20]

How to Incorporate the Outside View into Your Decisions

Kahneman and Amos Tversky, a psychologist who had a long collaboration with Kahneman, published a multistep process to help you use the outside view.[21] I have distilled their five steps into four and have added some thoughts. Here are the four steps:

1. *Select a reference class.* Find a group of situations, or a reference class, that is broad enough to be statistically significant but narrow enough to be useful in analyzing the decision that you face. The task is generally as much art as science, and is certainly trickier for problems that few people have dealt with before. But for decisions that are common—even if they are not common for you—identifying a reference class is straightforward. Mind the details. Take the example of mergers and acquisitions. We know that the shareholders of acquiring companies lose money in most mergers and acquisitions. But a closer look at the data reveals that the market responds more favorably to cash deals and those done at small premiums than to deals financed with stock at large premiums. So companies can improve their chances of making money from an acquisition by knowing what deals tend to succeed.

2. *Assess the distribution of outcomes.* Once you have a reference class, take a close look at the rate of success and failure. For example, fewer than one of six horses in Big
   Brown's position won the Triple Crown. Study the distribution and note the average outcome, the most common outcome, and extreme successes or failures.

   In his book *Full House*, Stephen Jay Gould, who was a
   paleontologist at Harvard University, showed the importance of knowing the distribution of outcomes after his doctor diagnosed him with mesothelioma. His doctor explained
   that half of the people diagnosed with the rare cancer lived
   only eight months (more technically, the median mortality
   was eight months), seemingly a death sentence. But Gould
   soon realized that while half the patients died within eight
   months, the other half went on to live much longer. Because
   of his relatively young age at diagnosis, there was a good
   chance he would be one of the fortunate ones. Gould wrote,
   "I had asked the right question and found the answers. I had
   obtained, in all probability, the most precious of all possible
   gifts in the circumstances—substantial time." Gould lived
   another twenty years.[22]

   Two other issues are worth mentioning. The statistical
   rate of success and failure must be reasonably stable over
   time for a reference class to be valid. If the properties of the
   system change, drawing inference from past data can be mis-
   leading. This is an important issue in personal finance,
   where advisers make asset allocation recommendations for
   their clients based on historical statistics. Because the statistical properties of markets shift over time, an investor can
   end up with the wrong mix of assets.

   Also keep an eye out for systems where small perturbations can lead to large-scale change. Since cause and effect
   are difficult to pin down in these systems, drawing on past
   experiences is more difficult. Businesses driven by hit products, like movies or books, are good examples. Producers

and publishers have a notoriously difficult time anticipating results, because success and failure is based largely on social influence, an inherently unpredictable phenomenon.

3. *Make a prediction.* With the data from your reference class in hand, including an awareness of the distribution of outcomes, you are in a position to make a forecast. The idea is to estimate your chances of success and failure. For all the reasons that I've discussed, the chances are good that your prediction will be too optimistic.

Sometimes when you find the right reference class, you see the success rate is not very high. So to improve your chance of success, you have to do something different than everyone else. One example is the play calling of National Football League coaches in critical game situations including fourth downs, kickoffs, and two-point conversion attempts. As in many other sports, conventional ways to decide about these situations are handed down from one generation of coaches to the next. But this stale decision-making process means scoring fewer points and winning fewer games.

Chuck Bower, an astrophysicist at Indiana University, and Frank Frigo, a former world backgammon champion, created a computer program called Zeus to assess the play-calling decisions of pro football coaches. Zeus uses the same modeling techniques that have succeeded in backgammon and chess programs, and the creators loaded it with statistics and the behavioral traits of coaches. Bower and Frigo found that only four teams in the thirty-two-team league made crucial decisions that agreed with Zeus over one-half of the time, and that nine teams made decisions that concurred less than one-quarter of the time. Zeus estimates that these poor decisions can cost a team more than one victory per year, a large toll in a sixteen-game season.

Most coaches stick to the conventional wisdom, because that is what they have learned and they are averse to the perceived negative consequences of breaking from past practice. But Zeus shows that the outside view can lead to more wins for the coach willing to break with tradition. This is an opportunity for coaches willing to think twice.[23]

4. *Assess the reliability of your prediction and fine-tune.* How good we are at making decisions depends a great deal on what we are trying to predict. Weather forecasters, for instance, do a pretty good job of predicting what the temperature will be tomorrow. Book publishers, on the other hand, are poor at picking winners, with the exception of those books from a handful of best-selling authors. The worse the record of successful prediction is, the more you should adjust your prediction toward the mean (or other relevant statistical measure). When cause and effect is clear, you can have more confidence in your forecast.

The main lesson from the inside-outside view is that while decision makers tend to dwell on uniqueness, the best decisions often derive from sameness. Don't get me wrong. I'm not advocating for bland, unimaginative, imitative, or risk-free decisions. I am saying there is a wealth of useful information based on situations that are similar to the ones that we face every day. We ignore that information to our own detriment. Paying attention to that wealth of information will help you make more effective decisions. Remember this discussion the next time a contender for the Triple Crown goes off at highly optimistic odds.

CHAPTER TWO

Open to Options

How Your Telephone Number Can
Influence Your Decisions

Daniel Kahneman's significant contributions to our under-standing of how people think and act should be a staple of any professional's training. During one meeting I had with him, his comment about the anchoring-and-adjustment heuristic really stuck with me. Here's an example of how this heuristic works, based on an exercise I did with my students at Columbia Business School. I gave them a form requesting two numbers.[1] If you have never done this exercise, take a moment and jot down your responses.

1. The last four digits of your phone number:

   _____

2. An estimate of the number of doctors in New York City's Manhattan borough:

   _____

The anchoring-and-adjustment heuristic has a bias, which predicts that the phone numbers will influence the doctor estimates. In my class, the students with phone numbers ending in 0000–2999 guessed an average of 16,531, while those with 7000–9999 reckoned 29,143, higher by 75 percent. Kahneman reported a similar pattern when he administered the test to his students. (As best as I can tell, there are approximately 20,000 doctors in Manhattan.)

Of course, individuals know that the last four digits of their phone number have nothing to do with the population of doctors in Manhattan, but the act of thinking about an arbitrary sum prior to making an estimate unleashes the powerful bias. What's also obvious is that the students would have most assuredly given a different estimate if I had reversed the order of the questions.

In deciding, people often start with a specific piece of information or trait (anchor) and adjust as necessary to come up with a final answer. The bias is for people to make insufficient adjustments from the anchor, leading to off-the-mark responses. Systematically, the final answer leans too close to the anchor, whether or not the anchor is sensible.[2]

But the point that Kahneman emphasized was that even if you explain anchoring to a group, it does not sink in. You can run an experiment right after a discussion of the concept and *still* see the bias in action. The main reason, psychologists believe, is that anchoring is predominantly subconscious.

Mental Models Rule Your World

Anchoring is symptomatic of this chapter's broader decision mistake: an insufficient consideration of alternatives. To be blunter, you can call it tunnel vision. Failure to entertain options or possibilities can lead to dire consequences, from a missed medical diagnosis to unwarranted confidence in a financial model. So what's going on in our heads that causes us to focus too narrowly?

One of my favorite explanations comes from Phillip Johnson-Laird, a psychologist known for his theory of mental models. Johnson-Laird argues that when we reason, "We use perception, the meanings of words and sentences, the significance of the propositions that they express, and our knowledge. Indeed, we use everything we've got to think of possibilities, and we represent each possibility in a mental model of the world."[3]

A few facets of Johnson-Laird's description bear emphasis. First, people reason from a set of premises and only consider compatible possibilities. As a result, people fail to consider what they believe is false. Consider a hand of cards, about which only one of the following three statements is true:

- It contains a king, an ace, or both.

- It contains a queen, an ace, or both.

- It contains a jack, a ten, or both.

Given these statements, can the hand contain an ace?

Johnson-Laird has presented this problem to many bright people, and most believe the answer is yes. But that is wrong. If there were an ace in the hand, the first two statements would be true, violating the condition that only one of the statements is true.[4] You can think of the premises and their alternatives as a beam of light that shines only on perceived possible outcomes, leaving lots of viable alternatives in the dark.

Second, and related, is the point that how a person sees a problem—how it's described to him, how he feels about it, and his individual knowledge—shapes how he reasons about it. Since we are poor logicians, a problem's presentation strongly influences how we choose. Prospect theory's findings over the last four decades, including common heuristics and associated biases, substantiate this point. We'll see a number of these biases in our tunnel-vision mistakes.

Last, a mental model is an internal representation of an external reality, an incomplete representation that trades detail for speed.[5] Once formed, mental models replace more cumbersome reasoning processes, but are only as good as their ability to match reality. An ill-suited mental model will lead to a decision-making fiasco.[6]

Our minds are just trying to get an answer—the proper diagnosis for a sick patient, the right price for an acquisition, what will happen next in a novel—and have routines to get the answer quickly and often efficiently. But getting the right solution expeditiously means homing in on what seems to us to be the most likely outcomes and leaving out a lot of what could be. For most of our evolutionary past, this worked well. But the causal patterns that worked in a natural environment tens of thousands of years ago often do not hold in today's technological world. So when the stakes are sufficiently high, we must slow down and swing the light over the full range of possible outcomes.

Content with the Plausible

Tunnel vision is the source of a slew of mistakes, and we need only look as far as the anchoring-and-adjustment heuristic, and its related bias, to see the first. Why don't people make sufficient adjustments from an anchor to come up with accurate estimates? Work by Nicholas Epley, a psychologist at the University of Chicago Business School, and Thomas Gilovich, a psychologist at Cornell University, suggests that we start with an anchor and then move toward the right answer. But most of us stop adjusting once we reach a value we deem plausible or acceptable.

In one experiment, the psychologists asked subjects to answer six questions that had natural anchors. For instance, they asked the participants to estimate the freezing point (degrees Fahrenheit) for vodka, where the natural anchor is thirty-two degrees, the freezing point for water. They then asked the subjects for a range specifying their highest and lowest plausible estimates. For the vodka question, the mean estimate was twelve degrees, and the range of values was from twenty-three to minus seven degrees (vodka freezes at minus twenty degrees). According to Epley and Gilovich, these results suggest that the adjustment from the anchor "entails a search for a plausible estimate" and that the subjects terminate the adjustment once they reach what they believe is a reasonable answer.[7]

You can also see the consequence of anchoring and adjustment in negotiation. Gregory Northcraft and Margaret Neale, psychologists who study negotiation tactics, presented a group of real estate agents identical background material on a specific house—its size, amenities, and recent comparable-house transactions. To measure the anchoring effect, the researchers gave some agents different listing prices for the same house. Sure enough, the agents who saw a high listing price appraised the house for substantially more than those who saw a low price (see figure 2-1). Notable, too, is that less than 20 percent of the agents reported using the listing price data in their appraisal, insisting instead their assessment was independent. This bias is pernicious in large part because we are so unaware of it.[8]

FIGURE 2-1

Real estate brokers subconsciously anchor on given values

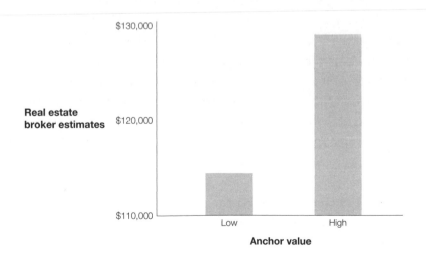

Source: Adapted from Gregory B. Northcraft and Margaret A. Neale, "Experts, Amateurs, and Real Estate: An Anchoring-and-Adjustment Perspective on Property Pricing Decisions," *Organizational Behavior and Human Decision Processes* 39, no. 1 (1987): 84–97.

Anchoring is relevant in high-stakes political or business negotiations. In situations with limited information or uncertainty, anchors can strongly influence the outcome. For instance, studies show that the party that makes the first offer can benefit from a strong anchoring effect in ambiguous situations. Developing and recognizing a full range of outcomes is the best protection against the anchoring effect if you are sitting on the other side of the negotiating table.[9]

Judging Books by Their Covers

In his book *How Doctors Think*, Dr. Jerome Groopman describes a trim and fit forest ranger who found himself in a hospital emergency room with chest pains. The doctor on duty listened carefully to the ranger's symptoms, reviewed a checklist for heart disease, and ordered some standard tests. All came out fine. The results, along with the man's healthy look, prompted the doctor to assure the patient there was an "about zero" chance his heart was the source of the problem.

The next day, the forest ranger came back in with a heart attack. Fortunately, he survived. But the doctor who had seen him the previous day was beside himself. On reflection, the doctor realized he had fallen prey to a bias that arises from the representativeness heuristic. This bias, the second of our decision mistakes, says we often rush to conclusions based on representative categories in our mind, neglecting possible alternatives. The well-worn aphorism "don't judge a book by its cover" speaks to this bias, encouraging us to remain open to options even as our mind seeks to shut them down. In this case, the doctor's error was to rule out a heart attack because the patient appeared to be a model of health and fitness. "You have to be prepared in your mind for the atypical and not so quickly reassure yourself, and the patient, that everything is okay," the doctor later mused.[10]

The availability heuristic, judging the frequency or probability of an event based on what is readily available in memory, poses a related challenge. We tend to give too much weight to the probability of something if we have seen it recently or if it is vivid in our mind. Groopman tells of a woman who came to the hospital suffering from a low-grade fever and a high respiratory rate. Her community had recently experienced a wave of viral pneumonia, creating mental availability for the physician. He diagnosed her as having a subclinical case, suggesting she had the pneumonia but that the symptoms had yet to surface. Instead, it turned out she had a case of aspirin toxicity. She had taken too many aspirin in an attempt to treat a cold, and her fever and respiratory rate were classic symptoms. But the doctor overlooked them because of the vividness of the viral pneumonia. Like representativeness, availability encourages us to ignore alternatives.[11]

Think carefully about how the representativeness and availability heuristics may impose on your decisions. Have you ever judged someone solely based on how he or she looks? Have you ever feared flying more after hearing of a plane crash? If the answer is yes, you are a normal human. But you also risk misunderstanding, or missing altogether, plausible outcomes.

Is the Trend Your Friend?

Let's play a little game. Look at a random sequence of squares and circles (figure 2-2). What shape do you expect next?

FIGURE 2-2

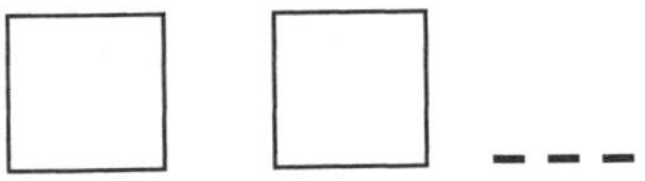

Source: Adapted from Jason Zweig, *Your Money and Your Brain: How the New Science of Neuroeconomics Can Help Make You Rich* (New York: Simon & Schuster, 2007).

The minds of most people strongly suggest the same answer: another square. This leads us to the third common mistake, a tendency to extrapolate inappropriately from past results. Scott Huettel, a psychologist and neuroscientist at Duke University, and his colleagues confirmed this finding when they placed subjects in a brain-reading functional magnetic resonance imaging (fMRI) machine and showed them random patterns of circles and squares. After one symbol, people did not know what to expect next. But after two in a row, they automatically expected a third, even though they knew the series was random. Two may not be a trend, but our brains sure think so.[12]

This mistake is tough because our minds have a deep-seated desire to make out patterns and our prediction process is very rapid (the researchers call it "automatic and obligatory"). This pattern recognition ability evolved through the millennia and was profoundly useful for most of human existence. "In a natural environment, almost all patterns are predictive," says Huettel. "For example, when you hear a crash behind you, it's not something artificial; it means that a branch is falling, and you need to get out of the way. So, we evolved to look for those patterns. But these causal relationships don't necessarily hold in the technological world that can produce irregularities, and in which we look for patterns where none exist."[13]

Extrapolation puts a finer point on a number of other mistakes as well. We can restate the problem of induction as inappropriately projecting into the future, based on a limited number of observations. Failure to reflect reversion to the mean is the result of extrapolating earlier performance into the future without giving proper weight to the role of chance. Models based on past results forecast in the belief that the future will be characteristically similar to history. In each case, our minds—or the models our minds construct—anticipate without giving suitable consideration to other possibilities.

When in Doubt, Rationalize Your Decision

Cognitive dissonance is one facet of our next mistake, the rigidity that comes with the innate human desire to be internally and externally consistent.[14] Cognitive dissonance, a theory developed in the 1950s by Leon Festinger, a social psychologist, arises when "a person holds two cognitions—ideas, attitudes, beliefs, opinions—that are psychologically inconsistent."[15] The dissonance causes mental discomfort that our minds seek to reduce.

Many times we resolve the discomfort by figuring out how to justify our actions, for example, the man who recognizes that wearing a seat belt improves safety but who doesn't do it. To reduce the dissonance, he may rationalize the decision by noting the seat belt is uncomfortable or by claiming that his above-average driving ability will keep him from harm's way. A little self-delusion is OK for most of us, because the stakes are generally low and it lets us sleep at night.

But self-justification is a big problem if the stakes are high. A scan of history shows the deplorable behavior of malevolent dictators, religious extremists, and cheating executives who justified their own behavior as they harmed others. Here are some examples that show the lengths the mind will go to in order to resolve internal conflict.

While other eighth graders hoped to be astronauts or firefighters, Kurt Wise dreamed of getting a PhD from Harvard and teaching at a big university. After receiving an undergraduate degree from the University of Chicago, Wise realized part of his dream by earning a doctorate at Harvard in geology as a student of Stephen Jay Gould, the well-known paleobiologist. Wise's thesis complemented the fossil record by offering a statistical method to infer the period in which a particular species lived, often millions of years ago. His contribution was fully consistent with well-established evolutionary theory.

Why mention Wise's credentials? In direct contradiction to his scientific training, Wise is a "young earth creationist," someone who believes the literal Bible account of God creating the earth only a few thousand years ago. The conflict in Wise's mind boiled to the point where he decided to painstakingly go through the Bible and cut out every verse that was inconsistent with evolutionary theory. The project took Wise months, and when he finished, the truth he dreaded was clear: there was not much left of the Bible. So he had to decide between evolution and scripture. He chose scripture. As he recounts, "It was there that night that I accepted the Word of God and rejected all that would ever counter it, including evolution." He went on, "If all of the evidence in the universe turned against creationism, I would be the first to admit it, but I would still be a creationist. Here I must stand."[16]

In the mid-1950s, a trio of scientists including Festinger took note of a small Illinois-based group that claimed to receive lessons from spiritual beings on other planets. The scientists infiltrated the group and gathered firsthand accounts of the meetings and events. Over time, the members came to believe that beings from outer space had shared an ominous foreboding about a world-destroying flood to occur on December 21. The good news was that spaceships would descend at midnight and rescue the cult's believers.

Prior to the doomsday date, the cult members displayed two seemingly contradictory behaviors. On one hand, they maintained or escalated their commitment to the group by quitting their jobs, stopping their studies, and giving away their possessions in anticipation of their new lives. On the other hand, they did little to help outsiders, beyond sharing vague news of impending disaster.

On the evening of December 20, the believers gathered at the house of Marian Keech, one of the group's spiritual leaders, waiting for the spacemen. When midnight came and passed, the members grew unsettled. During a break after 4 a.m., Thomas Armstrong, also a cult leader, confided in one of the infiltrators, "I don't care what happens tonight. I can't afford to doubt. I won't doubt even if we have to make an announcement to the press tomorrow and admit we were wrong."[17] Note the striking similarity between Wise's and Armstrong's comments.

Around 4:45 a.m., a message came to Mrs. Keech: the cult had been such a "force of Good" that the world was spared its awful fate. This provided a spark for the group's spirit, but a second missive shortly thereafter made an even bigger difference. The cult was to release this "Christmas message" to the newspapers immediately and in complete detail. So the exhausted members, led by Mrs. Keech, started calling newspapers, radio stations, and wire services. From then on, the cult opened up. "The house was crowded with the now-welcome horde of newspaper, radio, and television representatives," the scientists wrote, "and visitors streamed in and out the door."[18]

While cognitive dissonance is about internal consistency, the confirmation bias is about external consistency. The confirmation bias occurs when an individual seeks information that confirms a prior belief or view and disregards, or disconfirms, evidence that counters it.[19] Robert Cialdini, a social psychologist at Arizona State University, notes that consistency offers two benefits. First, it permits us to stop thinking about an issue, giving us a mental break. Second, consistency frees us from the consequence of reason—namely, changing our behavior. The first allows us to avoid thinking; the second to avoid acting.[20]

When radio became popular in the 1920s and 1930s in the United States, some psychologists worried that the media would infect a vulnerable public with ideas. The fear was that everyone hearing the same message simultaneously might spark some massive, unintended, coordinated behavior. Elihu Katz and Paul Lazarsfeld, prominent sociologists, refuted this view. Their work showed that people pretty much kept on doing what they were doing before, irrespective of the media.[21]

When Katz and Lazarsfeld studied why the media had such a muted influence on individuals, they discovered that people are selective in their exposure and retention. In effect, most people see and hear what they want and tune out everything else. For example, a government memo explained the demands of former Vice President Dick Cheney when he went to a hotel. These included four cans of Diet Sprite, a pot of decaffeinated coffee, a room temperature of sixty-eight degrees, and all televisions tuned to Fox News, the channel that most closely reflected his views.[22] This facet of the confirmation bias, selective exposure and retention, minimizes our exposure to diverse ideas.

Drew Westen, a psychologist at Emory University, and his colleagues did a study of selective exposure and retention among political partisans. The researchers gave staunch Democrats and Republicans surveys and later put them in an fMRI machine and scanned their brains as they read slides. The statements included clearly inconsistent comments from Democratic and Republican presidential candidates and some politically neutral people.

The partisans had no problem seeing the contradictions in the opposition candidate, giving scores near four on a four-point discrepancy rating. But when their own candidate was inconsistent, the average discrepancy rating was closer to two, suggesting they saw

FIGURE 2-3

Partisans notice discrepancies in the other party but not in their own

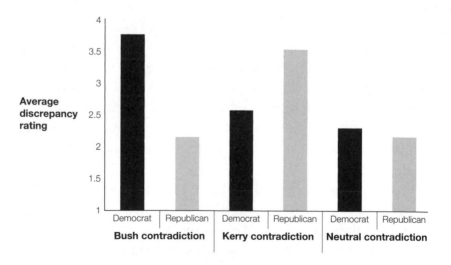

Source: Drew Westen, Pavel S. Blagov, Keith Harenski, Clint Kilts, and Stephan Hamann, "Neural Bases of Motivated Reasoning: An fMRI Study of Emotional Constraints on Partisan Political Judgment in the 2004 U.S. Presidential Election," Journal of Cognitive Neuroscience 18, no. 11 (2006): 1951.

minimal contradiction. Finally, neither Democrats nor Republicans reacted strongly to the neutral contradictions (see figure 2-3).[23]

The brain images were equally revealing and followed a similar pattern. When the partisans saw information they didn't agree with, none of the circuits involved in conscious reasoning were very active. But when they saw what they liked, their brains eliminated negative emotional states and activated positive ones. The brains of the partisans massively reinforced what they already believed.[24]

The study of political partisans shows the large role that attention plays in tunnel vision. Paying a lot of attention to one thing means you are not paying a lot of attention to others, often creating a form of blindness. Every year, I show a video to my class that demonstrates this phenomenon. Daniel Simons and Christopher Chabris, psychologists who study perception, created the now famous thirty-second video that shows two teams, one wearing white shirts and the other black, in a nondescript lobby. Each team passes a basketball back and forth. I ask the students to count the number of passes the white team makes, which is somewhat challenging because the players move around. Of course, the students know there's some trick, so they concentrate their attention on the task.

There is a trick. Roughly halfway through the video, a woman wearing a gorilla suit walks into the middle of the scene, thumps her chest, and walks off. Less than 60 percent of students concentrating on the challenging visual task notice the gorilla (see figure 2-4). I then rerun the video and ask the students to watch it unencumbered by the task. There are always nervous chuckles when the gorilla makes her appearance. My results are very consistent with what other experimenters report.

Let's face it: we all have finite attention bandwidths. If you dedicate all that bandwidth to one task, none is left over for anything else. So people should be alert to striking a balance between nitty-gritty problem solving and a broader context.[25]

There's something else that contributes to tunnel vision, and it's something we can all relate to in varying degrees—stress. Like a lot of things in life, a little bit of stress (or a lot for a very short time) is a good thing. But too much stress can muddle our thinking by clipping our ability to think long term.

Stress is often very helpful. The classic stress response mobilizes energy to your muscles by increasing your heart rate, blood pressure, and breathing. High stress also helps your sensory system. For example, policemen report that during shootouts their visual acuity and focus improves, they sense a slowdown in time, and they fail to hear sounds. For a short burst, the mind can focus intently on the task at hand. This reaction is valuable in extraordinary circumstances.[26]

Stress is bad, however, if it is constant. Animals have a stress response when they are faced with physical threats—imagine a lion is chasing a zebra—but calm down once the threat passes. While humans are periodically threatened physically, most of our stress comes from the emotional strains of job deadlines, financial worries, and relationship issues. Crucially, the stress response is the same whether it comes from physical or psychological provocation. And, unlike most of the animal kingdom, we can experience chronic psychological stress. Events turn on our stress response system and we can't turn it off. While mobilizing your body to respond to a

FIGURE 2-4

A majority of viewers fail to see the gorilla

Source: D. J. Simons and C. F. Chabris, "Gorillas in our midst: Sustained inattentional blindness for dynamic events," *Perception* 28 (1999): 1059–1074. Figure provided by Daniel Simons. The video depicted in this figure is available as part of a DVD from Viscog Productions (http://www.viscog.com).

short-term threat is an amazing feat, the same response is deeply detrimental to your health if it is always on.

Robert Sapolsky, a neurobiologist at Stanford University and an expert on stress, notes that an important feature of the stress response is that it turns off long-term systems. You need not worry about your digestion, growth, disease prevention, or reproduction if you are about to be a lion's lunch. The stress response is, in Sapolsky's words, "penny-wise and dollar foolish." And this plays into tunnel vision.

Stressed people struggle to think about the long term. The manager about to lose her job tomorrow has little interest in making a decision that will make her better off in three years. Psychological stress creates a sense of immediacy that inhibits consideration of options with distant payoffs. The stress response, so effective for dealing with here-and-now risks, co-opts the decision-making apparatus and compels poor decisions.[27]

Incentives, or What's in It for Me?

Incentives matter, as economists have argued quite compellingly. An incentive is any factor, financial or otherwise, that encourages a particular decision or action. In many situations, incentives create a conflict of interest that compromises a person's ability to properly consider alternatives. So when you evaluate your own decisions or the decisions of others, consider the choices that the incentives encourage.

Dr. Katrina Firlik, a neurosurgeon, shared an example: at conference dealing with spine surgery, a surgeon presented the case of a female patient with a herniated disc in her neck and pain that was caused by a pinched nerve. She had already failed typical conservative treatments such as physical therapy, medication, and waiting it out.

The surgeon asked the audience to vote on a couple of choices for surgery. The first was the newer anterior approach, where the surgeon removes the entire disc, replaces it with a bone plug, and fuses the discs. The vast majority of the hands shot up. The second choice was the older posterior approach, where the surgeon removes only the portion of the disc that is compressing the nerve. No fusion is required because the procedure leaves most of the disc intact. Only a few audience members raised their hands.

The speaker then asked the audience, which was almost entirely male, "What if this patient is your wife?" The show of hands was reversed for the same two choices. The main reason is that the amount surgeons are paid for the newer and more complicated procedure is typically several times what they'd receive for the older procedure.[28]

Incentives also played a central role in the financial crisis of 2007–2009. Take the subprime mortgage market, which was "undeniably the original source of crisis," according to Alan Greenspan, former chairman of the Federal Reserve. People unable to meet prime credit standards because of a poor or limited credit history were able to borrow unprecedented amounts of money, often at low initial interest rates. Subprime mortgages went from about 10 percent of new mortgages in the late 1990s to 20 percent by 2006, and unregulated lenders represented the bulk of that volume. These subprime borrowers were the first to run into trouble when home prices dropped, triggering a cascade of losses throughout the financial system.

While letting the subprime mortgage market grow as it did was clearly bad, incentives for the participants strongly encouraged it. For example:

- People with poor credit standards could own the nice homes they coveted.

- Lenders earned fees on the loans that they made, encouraging them to relax underwriting standards. They also did not hold on to the mortgages for the most part, so their incentives were primarily to grow rather than to lend prudently.

- Investment banks bought the individual mortgages and bundled them for resale to other investors, earning a fee.

- Rating agencies were paid a fee to rate the mortgage-backed securities. They issued a good number of AAA-ratings, suggesting a high level of creditworthiness.

- Investors in AAA-rated mortgage-backed securities earned higher returns than they did on other AAA issues. Since many of those investors were paid based on portfolio performance, the additional yield led to higher fees.[29]

The subprime mess revealed that what may appear to be optimal for the individual agents in a complex system may be suboptimal for the system as a whole. Even in the wake of the debacle, we can easily see the motivations of each constituent in the chain: more homes, more fees, more yield. On one level, those motivations make sense. But when all the participants pursued their goals without giving thought to the broader impact on the housing markets and the financial system, the system collapsed. For fervent believers in markets, this collective failure was especially stunning. Greenspan wrote, "Those of us who have looked to the self-interest of lending institutions to protect shareholder's equity (myself included) are in a state of shocked disbelief."[30]

Many poor decisions result from inappropriate incentives rather than mistakes. The biases that come with incentives are often subconscious. Max Bazerman, a professor at the Harvard Business School who studies decision making, and some fellow researchers asked over one hundred accountants to review five ambiguous accounting vignettes and to judge the accounting for each. Half the accountants were told that they had been hired by the company, and the rest were told they were hired by a different company. Those who played the role of auditor for the company were 30 percent more likely to find the choices compliant with accounting principles, suggesting that even a hypothetical relationship with the company shaped judgment. The researchers wrote, "Perhaps the most notable feature of the psychological processes at work in conflicts of interest is that they can occur without any conscious intention to indulge in corruption." Incentives are a strong contributor to tunnel vision.[31]

How do you avoid the tunnel vision trap? Here's a five-point checklist:

1. *Explicitly consider alternatives.* As Johnson-Laird's model of reasoning suggests, decision makers often fail to consider a sufficient number of alternatives. You should examine a full range of alternatives, using base rates or market-derived guidelines when appropriate to mitigate the influence of the representativeness or availability biases.

   To this end, negotiation teachers suggest entering talks knowing your best alternative to a negotiated agreement, your walkaway price, and the same two sums for the party across the table. These figures allow you to improve the odds of an advantageous deal and to avoid being surprised. In other settings, too, enumerating your alternatives clearly and completely is very helpful.[32]

2. *Seek dissent.* Much easier said than done, the idea is to prove your views wrong. There are a couple of techniques. The first is to ask questions that could elicit answers that might contradict your own views. Then listen carefully to the answers. Do the same when canvassing data: look for reliable sources that offer conclusions different than yours. This helps avoid a foolish inconsistency.[33]

   When possible, surround yourself with people who have dissenting views. This is emotionally and intellectually very difficult, but is highly effective in exposing alternatives. It also reduces the risk of group think, when group members try to reach consensus with minimal conflict by avoiding testing alternative ideas. Abraham Lincoln embodied this approach. After his unlikely ascent to the White House,

Lincoln appointed a number of his eminent foes to cabinet positions. He ended up winning the respect of his former adversaries, as his team of rivals navigated the United States through the Civil War.[34]

3. *Keep track of previous decisions.* We humans have an odd tendency: once an event has passed, we believe we knew more about the outcome beforehand than we really did. This is known as hindsight bias. The research shows people are unreliable in recalling how an uncertain situation appeared to them before finding out the results.

   My family was driving to the airport to catch a flight for a vacation. We could have gone either on Interstate 95 or on the Merritt Parkway, two roughly equivalent routes. I listened to the traffic report, heard both were clear, and picked Interstate 95. A few minutes later, we ran into traffic caused by an accident. After clearing the traffic, we dashed to the airport, only to narrowly miss our flight. My wife turned to me and in an exasperated tone said, "I *knew* we should have taken the Merritt." As Søren Kierkegaard, the Danish philosopher said, "Life must be understood backwards . . . But it must be lived—forwards."[35]

   So we generally fail to consider enough alternatives looking forward and think we knew what was going on looking backward. The antidote to both is to write down the rationale behind decisions and to consistently revisit past actions. A decision-making journal is a cheap and easy routine to offset hindsight bias and encourage a fuller view of possibilities.

4. *Avoid making decisions while at emotional extremes.* Making decisions under ideal conditions is tough enough, but you can be sure your decision-making skills will rapidly erode if you are emotionally charged. Stress, anger, fear, anxiety, greed, and euphoria are all mental states antithetical to

quality decisions. But just as it's hard to make good decisions during emotional upheaval, it's also hard to make good decisions in the absence of emotion. Antonio Damasio, a neuroscientist, suggests that "our reason can operate most efficiently" when we have some emotional poise. Whenever possible, try to postpone important decisions if you feel at an emotional extreme.[36]

5. *Understand incentives.* Consider carefully what incentives exist, and what behaviors the incentives might motivate. Financial incentives are generally easy to spot, but nonfinancial incentives, like reputation or fairness, are less obvious yet still important in driving decisions. While few of us believe that incentives distort our decisions, the evidence shows that the effect can be subconscious. Finally, what may be individually good for group members can be destructive for the group overall.

For various psychological reasons, humans tend to consider too few alternatives when making decisions. In many cases, the most obvious choice is the right choice. But in a world that presents more alternatives than it used to, tunnel vision can lead to substantial but entirely avoidable mistakes. Here again, you need not labor over every decision. Rather, when the stakes are sufficiently high, ask whether you are susceptible to tunnel vision. If so, scrutinize your decision-making process and take concrete steps to intelligently consider hidden possibilities.

CHAPTER THREE

The Expert Squeeze

Why Netflix Knows More Than Clerks Do About Your

Favorite Films

A CCURATELY PROJECTING HOLIDAY SALES is a crucial task for retailers. A forecast that is too low leaves shelves bare and profits lost, while too much optimism leads to dusty inventory and pressure on profit margins. So retailers have a great incentive to come up with a precise sales estimate. To do so, most merchants rely on experts—individuals in the organization who gather information, study trends, and make predictions.

The stakes are especially high for consumer electronics firms because they generate so much of their revenue during the gift-giving season and the value of their inventory depreciates rapidly. The pressure is really on the internal experts at consumer-electronics giant Best Buy, one of a multitude of retailers that rely on specialists. So you can imagine the reaction when James Surowiecki, author of the best-selling book *The Wisdom of Crowds*, strolled into Best Buy's headquarters and delivered a startling message: a relatively uninformed crowd could predict better than the firm's best seers.[1]

Surowiecki's message resonated with Jeff Severts, an executive then running Best Buy's gift-card business. Severts wondered whether the idea would really work in a corporate setting, so he gave a few hundred people in the organization some basic background information and asked them to forecast February 2005 gift-card sales. When he tallied the results in March, the average of the nearly two hundred respondents was 99.5 percent accurate. His team's official forecast was off by five percentage points. The crowd was better, but was it a fluke?

Later that year, Severts set up a central location for employees to submit and update their estimates of sales from Thanksgiving through year-end. More than three hundred employees participated, and Severts kept track of the crowd's collective guess. When the dust settled in early 2006, he revealed that the official August forecast of the internal experts was 93 percent accurate, while the presumed amateur crowd was off by only one-tenth of 1 percent.[2]

Best Buy subsequently allocated additional resources to its prediction market, called TagTrade.[3] The market has yielded useful insights for managers through the more than two thousand employees who have made tens of thousands of trades on topics ranging from customer satisfaction scores to store openings to movie sales. For instance, in early 2008, TagTrade indicated that sales of a new service package for laptops would be disappointing when compared with the formal forecast. When early results confirmed the prediction, the company pulled the offering and relaunched it in the fall. While far from flawless, the prediction market has been more accurate than the experts a majority of the time and has provided management with information it would not have had otherwise.[4]

Sommeliers, Don't Sniff at This Equation

When it comes to wine, I am an ignoramus. While I enjoy a glass with my dinner, I almost always defer to a waiter or dining partner for a wine selection and naively associate pleasantness with price.[5] Judging wine strikes me as similar to viewing art—the beauty is in the taste buds of the beholder—and I have always viewed the swirl, sip, and swish crowd as erudite and a bit mysterious. So imagine my delight when Ian Ayres, an econometrician and law professor at Yale University, included an equation in his book *Super Crunchers* that promised to reveal the value of wine without having to take a swig:[6]

$$\text{Wine value} = -12.14540 + 0.00117 \text{ winter rainfall} + 0.61640$$
$$\text{average growing season temperature} - 0.00386 \text{ harvest rainfall}$$

Orley Ashenfelter, an economist and wine enthusiast, calculated this regression equation to explain the quality of red wines from France's Bordeaux region. The Bordeaux vintners have long produced wines using consistent methods and have kept conscientious records of rainfall and temperature, providing Ashenfelter with plentiful data. Seeing a clear causal relationship between weather and wine quality, he generated the equation to quantify the link. Despite being scorned by the inner sanctum of the wine cognoscenti, Ashenfelter's value predictions have proven remarkably accurate and particularly useful in judging young wines.[7]

In this case, computers outperform connoisseurs. For years, wine drinkers had to rely on the opinions of experts who themselves vary in quality and consistency. It took an outsider—an economist at that—to identify previously overlooked relationships. With the equation in hand, the computer can deliver appraisals that are quicker, cheaper, more reliable, and without a whiff of snobbishness.

Fall of the House of Experts

As networks harness the wisdom of crowds and computing power grows, the ability of experts to add value in their predictions is steadily declining. I call this the *expert squeeze*, and evidence for it is mounting. Despite this trend, we still pine for experts—individuals with special skill or know-how—believing that many forms of knowledge are technical and specialized. We openly defer to people in white lab coats or pinstripe suits, believing they hold the answers, and we harbor misgivings about computer-generated outcomes or the collective opinion of a bunch of tyros.[8]

The expert squeeze means that people stuck in old habits of thinking are failing to use new means to gain insight into the problems they face. Knowing when to look beyond experts requires a totally fresh point of view, and one that does not come naturally. To be sure, the future for experts is not all bleak. Experts retain an advantage in some crucial areas. The challenge is to know when and how to use them.

So how do you, as a decision maker, manage the expert squeeze? The first step: carefully consider the problem you face. Figure 3-1 helps to guide this process. The second column from the left covers problems that have rules-based solutions with limited possible outcomes. Here, someone can investigate the problem based on past patterns and write down rules to guide decisions.[9] Experts do well with these tasks, but once the principles are clear and well defined, computers are cheaper and more reliable. Think of tasks such as

FIGURE 3-1

The value of experts

Domain description	Rule based; limited range of outcomes	Rule based; wide range of outcomes	Probabilistic; limited range of outcomes	Probabilistic; wide range of outcomes
Expert performance	Worse than computers	Generally better than computers	Equal to or worse than collectives	Worse than collectives
Expert agreement	High	Moderate	Moderate/Low	Low
Examples	• Credit scoring • Simple medical diagnosis	• Chess • Go	• Admissions officers • Poker	• Stock market • Economy

credit scoring or simple forms of medical diagnosis. Experts agree about how to approach these problems because the solutions are transparent and for the most part tried and true.

Experts are initially important for these problems because they figure out the rules, or algorithms, that work. Think of Ashenfelter. Yet the underlying order is not always obvious. Sometimes experts must use statistical methods to find structure in the system, but once they do, the silicon can take over.

The experience of Harrah's Casino in the early 2000s is a good illustration. For years, Harrah's, like other casinos, fawned over people who played at the high-stakes tables—the high rollers. However, a careful study of customer data revealed it was the middle-aged and senior adults with discretionary time and income who added the most value. So the executives used the data to create even greater loyalty from their best customers, while still managing the high rollers effectively. The conventional wisdom that the expert executives had perpetuated—that high rollers were the highest value customers—was flat wrong, but only revealed by a new look at the data.[10]

Now let's go to the opposite extreme, the column on the far right that deals with probabilistic fields with a wide range of outcomes. Here are no simple rules. You can only express possible outcomes in probabilities, and the range of outcomes is wide. Examples include economic and political forecasts. The evidence shows that collectives outperform experts in solving these problems. For instance, economists are extremely poor forecasters of interest rates, often failing to accurately guess the direction of rate moves, much less their correct level.[11] Note, too, that not only are experts poor at predicting actual outcomes, they rarely agree with one another. Two equally credentialed experts may make opposite predictions and, hence, decisions from one another.

One example is the forecasting of oil prices. In one camp are experts like Matthew Simmons, an investment banker and consultant specializing in energy, who argues that the world has reached its peak of oil extraction and that oil prices are likely to rise as a consequence. In the other camp are experts including Daniel Yergin, an economic researcher, who argues that technology will make it possible to find new sources of oil and to extract them profitably. Both camps have smart and persuasive experts but come to opposite conclusions about the direction of future prices.[12]

The middle two columns are the remaining province for experts. Experts do well with rules-based problems with a wide range of outcomes because they are better than computers at eliminating bad choices and making creative connections between bits of information. Eric Bonabeau, a physicist who now consults with businesses, has developed programs that combine computers and experts to find solutions for packaging design. Bonabeau uses the computer to generate alternatives using the principles of evolution (recombination and mutation) and has experts select the best designs for the next generation (selection). The computers are effective at creating the design alternatives but have no taste. Large consumer product companies including Procter & Gamble and Pepsi-Cola have successfully used this technique to make their products stand out.[13]

Still, computers will continue to make inroads into this column as their performance improves. Consider that until relatively recently, no computer could beat the world chess champion. But Deep Blue, IBM's chess-playing supercomputer, beat Garry Kasparov, the world champion from 1985 to 2000, in a six-game match in 1999. Yet humans still dominate computer programs in the game of Go, which has simple rules but allows many more position combinations than chess because of its larger nineteen-by-nineteen board. Here it is only a matter of time. As computing power becomes greater and cheaper, silicon will win this battle as well. Table 3-1 shows how computers stack up versus humans in various games.

For problems that are probabilistic with a limited range of outcomes, the verdict for experts is mixed. Computers and crowds fare poorly if they lack domain-specific knowledge. For instance, an expert coach will probably create a better game plan than a computer because he can draw on the unique knowledge of his team and the competition. Similarly, an executive may be able to better shape strategy for her corporation.[14]

TABLE 3-1

Man versus machine: Where is the advantage?

	ADVANTAGE	
Game	**Machine**	**Man**
Bridge		X
Checkers	X	
Chess	X	
Go		X
Othello	X	
Scrabble	X	

Source: Matthew L. Ginsberg, "Computers, Games and the Real World," *Scientific American Presents: Exploring Intelligence* 9, no. 4 (1998): 84–89.

Once you have properly classified a problem, turn to the best method for solving it. As we will see, computers and collectives remain underutilized guides for decision making across a host of realms including medicine, business, and sports. That said, experts remain vital in three capacities. First, experts must create the very systems that replace them. Severts helped design the prediction market that outperforms Best Buy's in-house forecasters. Until Ashenfelter came along, evaluating Bordeaux's red wines was in large part subjective. Of course, the experts must stay on top of these systems, improving the market or equation as need be.

Next, we need experts for strategy. I mean strategy broadly, including not only day-to-day tactics but also the ability to trouble-shoot by recognizing interconnections as well as the creative process of innovation, which involves combining ideas in novel ways. Decisions about how best to challenge a competitor, which rules to enforce, or how to recombine existing building blocks to create novel products or experiences are jobs for experts.

Finally, we need people to deal with people. A lot of decision making involves psychology as much as it does statistics. A leader must understand others, make good decisions, and encourage others to buy in to the decision.

The Clerk Can't Match Cinematch

When my wife and I lived in New York City in the early 1990s, we supplemented our evenings at the movies with jaunts to the local video store. Like others of that era, the store had a couple of employees who would gladly recommend films based on what you liked before and what mood you were in, and who might even throw in an off-the-beaten-path title from time to time. These employees were quite helpful, considering they were working with a relatively modest movie inventory and limited knowledge of our cinematic tastes.

Netflix, a Web-based DVD-rental firm founded in 1997, realized early on that successfully matching subscribers to movies was central to customer satisfaction—and hence the vibrancy of the business. In 2000, the company launched a service called Cinematch, a program of algorithms that pairs viewers and discs. Using consumer feedback, Cinematch rapidly improved its ability to anticipate consumer tastes and now drives well over half of Netflix's rentals, keeping users happy and reducing reliance on new releases. But the company's executives realized that Cinematch did not have all the answers. So in 2006, they issued a challenge: Netflix will pay a $1 million prize for a program that predicts consumer preferences 10 percent better than Cinematch.

As I write this, the Netflix Prize is still up for grabs, with the leading group 9.80 percent better than Cinematch. Two points bear emphasis. First, some really great minds are toiling on a problem that is worth a lot less to them than it is to Netflix. (Netflix executives freely admit that a winning algorithm is worth more than $1 million.) Second, Cinematch, or whatever program ultimately unseats it, is vastly better than the video-store employee in New York City.[15]

The night-and-day contrast between the quality of advice from Netflix's algorithms and the local video-store clerk illustrates this chapter's first decision mistake: using experts instead of mathematical models. This mistake, I admit, is hard to swallow and is a direct affront to experts of all stripes. But it is also among the best documented findings in the social sciences.

In 1954, Paul Meehl, a psychologist at the University of Minnesota, published a book that reviewed studies comparing the clinical judgment of experts (psychologists and psychiatrists) with linear statistical models. He made sure the analysis was done carefully so he could be confident that the comparisons were fair. In study after study, the statistical methods exceeded or matched the expert performance.[16] More recently, Philip Tetlock, a psychologist at the University of California, Berkeley, completed an exhaustive study of expert predictions, including twenty-eight thousand forecasts made by three hundred experts hailing from sixty countries over fifteen years. Tetlock asked the experts to predict political and economic outcomes, probabilistic fields with wide ranges of outcomes. Summarizing his results, Tetlock stated flatly, "It is impossible to find any domain in which humans clearly outperformed crude extrapolation algorithms, less still sophisticated statistical ones."[17]

Despite this decades-old and well-substantiated evidence, the practice of relying on experts in a wide range of domains has changed very little. The fact is most people have difficulty assimilating broad statistical evidence into the judgment at hand. When you face a decision, ask yourself whether you would rather get your next recommendation from Cinematch or the guy behind the video-store counter. You now know where you are most likely to get the most viewing pleasure.

What Jelly Beans Reveal About the Wisdom
of the Crowd

The Best Buy example, where a collection of partially informed nonexperts did better than experts, shows our second decision mistake: relying on experts instead of the wisdom of crowds. Understanding why collectives are often wise—and sometimes very unwise—requires us to look under the hood at how the wisdom of crowds works. But before proceeding, give the question some thought. How is it that a group of nonexperts can predict better than the resident expert?

Scott Page, a social scientist who has studied problem solving by groups, offers a very useful approach for understanding collective decision making. He calls it the diversity prediction theorem, which states:[18]

Collective error = average individual error − prediction diversity

The theorem uses squared errors as an accuracy measure, which researchers in the social sciences and statistics commonly employ because it assures that negative and positive errors do not cancel out.[19]

The average individual error captures the accuracy of the individual guesses. You can think of it as a measure of ability. Prediction diversity reflects the dispersion of guesses, or how different they are. The collective error, of course, is simply the difference between the correct answer and the average guess. Page discusses the diversity prediction theorem in depth in his book *The Difference*, and provides numerous examples of the theorem in action.

I illustrate the diversity prediction theorem by asking students to guess the number of jellybeans in a jar and showing them the collective error, average individual error, and the prediction diversity. For example, one year the average guess of the students was 1,151 jellybeans when the actual number was 1,116, an error of approximately 3 percent. The average individual was off by about 700 beans (and the guesses did not fall along a bell-shaped distribution). But the diversity was high enough to offset most of the individual errors, leaving a small collective error.

The diversity prediction theorem tells us that a diverse crowd will always predict more accurately than the average person in the crowd. Not sometimes. Always. This suggests that modesty is in order, but most people do not think of themselves as average—and certainly not as below average. Yet in reality, half of all people must be below average, and so you should sort out when you are likely to be one of them.

Also important is that collective accuracy is equal parts ability and diversity. You can reduce the collective error either by increasing ability or by increasing diversity. Both ability and diversity are essential. This implication is relevant for gauging the health of markets or building a successful team.[20]

Finally, while not a formal implication of the theorem, the collective is often better than even the best individual. So a diverse collective always beats the average person and frequently beats everyone. In the jellybean experiment, just two of the seventy-three students did better than the consensus. This is not good news for experts and deeply humbling for all decision makers.

With the diversity prediction theorem in hand, we can flesh out when crowds predict well. Three conditions must be in place: diversity, aggregation, and incentives. Each condition clicks into the equation. Diversity reduces the collective error. Aggregation assures that the market considers everyone's information. Incentives help reduce individual errors by encouraging people to participate only when they think they have an insight.

Clearly, collectives cannot solve all problems. If your plumbing is in need of repair, you are better off with a plumber than an English literature major, a Peace Corps volunteer, and an astrophysicist working together. But collectives are typically more valuable than experts when the problem is complex and specifiable rules cannot solve it.

Trust Your Blink Only If You Practice Blinking

In a recent survey, almost one-half of *Fortune* 1,000 executives said that they rely on intuition to make decisions. Indeed, best-selling books have fêted intuition, and business and medical lore holds intuitive (and seemingly enigmatic) decisions in special esteem.[21]

There is just one problem: intuition does not work all the time. This idea introduces our third decision mistake, inappropriately relying on intuition. Intuition can play a clear and positive role in decision making. The goal is to recognize when your intuition will serve you well versus when it will lead you astray.

Consider the two systems of decision making that Daniel Kahneman describes in his 2002 Nobel Prize lecture. System 1, the experiential system, is "fast, automatic, effortless, associative, and difficult to control or modify." System 2, the analytical system, is "slower, serial, effortful, and deliberately controlled."

In Kahneman's model, System 1 uses perception and intuition to generate impressions of objects or problems. These impressions are involuntary, and an individual may not be able to explain them. Kahneman argues that System 2 is involved in all judgments, whether or not the individual makes the decision consciously. So intuition is a judgment that reflects an impression.[22]

Through substantial, deliberate practice in a particular domain, experts can train and populate their experiential systems. So a chess master can size up the positions on the board very quickly, and an athlete knows what to do in a certain game situation. Effectively, the experts internalize the salient features of the system they are dealing with, freeing attention for higher-level, analytical thinking. This explains a number of the universal characteristics of experts, including the following:[23]

- Experts perceive patterns in their areas of expertise.

- Experts solve problems much faster than novices do.

- Experts represent problems at a deeper level than novices do.

- Experts can solve problems qualitatively.

Intuition therefore works well in stable environments, where conditions remain largely unchanged (e.g., the chess board and pieces), where feedback is clear, and where cause-and-effect relationships are linear. Intuition fails when you are dealing with a changing system, especially one that has phase transitions. Despite its near-magical connotation, intuition is losing relevance in an increasingly complex world.

Let me re-emphasize one point. I suggested that people become experts by using deliberate practice to train their experiential systems. Deliberate practice has a very specific meaning: it includes activities designed to improve performance, has repeatable tasks, incorporates high-quality feedback, and is not much fun. Most people—even alleged experts—do not come close to satisfying the conditions of deliberate practice and, accordingly, do not develop the necessary abilities for reliable intuition.[24]

How Homogeneity Contributes to the Whims of the Crowd

Now that I have extolled the virtues of computers and crowds, let me sound a warning in this chapter's final mistake: leaning too much on either formula-based approaches or the wisdom of crowds. While computers and collectives can be very useful, they do not warrant blind faith.

An example of overreliance on numbers is what Malcolm Gladwell calls the mismatch problem.[25] The problem, which you will immediately recognize, occurs when experts use ostensibly objective measures to anticipate future performance. In many cases, experts rely on measures that have little or no predictive value.

One prominent illustration of the mismatch problem is professional sports combines. A number of leagues gather the top amateur prospects prior to the draft and, under the careful watch of team scouts, cycle them through a series of tests designed to assess skills. These include physical tasks like weightlifting, running, and agility drills as well as psychological tests. The organizers then rank each player based on their performance. In some cases, a relatively good or bad showing meaningfully affects a player's draft position and hence his future expected earnings. Combines are stressful, costly, and time-consuming.

But in a detailed review of National Football League results, Frank Kuzmits and Arthur Adams, professors of business, found no consistent relationship between combine rankings and subsequent performance (there was one exception; sprinting speed helps predict the performance of running backs).[26] The results from hockey and basketball combines are similar. While quantitative and standardized, the results simply measure the wrong things.

Gladwell argues that the mismatch problem extends well beyond sports. He cites examples from education (credentials are poor predictors of performance), the legal profession (individuals accepted to law school under lower affirmative-action standards do as well as their classmates after graduation), and law enforcement (burly police officers may not be best for a largely relational job). You can easily see how the problem extends to interviews for all kinds of jobs, because the questions and answers rarely shed any light on prospective performance.

Unchecked devotion to the wisdom of crowds is also folly. While free-market devotees argue that prices reflect the most accurate assessments available, markets are extremely fallible. That is because when one or more of the three wisdom-of-crowds conditions are violated, the collective error can swell. Not surprisingly, diversity is the most likely condition to fail because we are inherently social and imitative. The pumped-up probability that Big Brown would win the Belmont Stakes in 2008 is a good example of a diversity breakdown, as are the excesses of the late 1990s stock market in the dot-com era and the financial crisis of 2007–2009.

Scientists have made good headway in understanding the processes that lead to diversity breakdowns. For example, information cascades occur when people make decisions based on the actions of others, rather than on their own private information. These cascades help explain booms, fads, fashions, and crashes. Social network theory, the study of how individuals or organizations are interconnected, provides a framework for understanding how these cascades propagate across large populations.[27]

Diversity breakdowns also occur in smaller groups. If you have ever been part of a committee, jury, or working team, you have likely seen this. The loss of diversity usually stems from a dominant leader, an absence of facts, or cognitive homogeneity in the group. To illustrate the latter, Cass Sunstein, a professor at the Harvard Law School, and some colleagues separated liberals and conservatives into like-minded groups and had them deliberate on socially controversial issues like same-sex marriages and affirmative action. In most cases, the group settled on a more extreme view than that expressed by most individuals in interviews conducted before the deliberations. The views of the individuals became more homogeneous after they spent time with their groups. Without diversity, collectives large or small can be wildly off the mark.[28]

So what can you do to make the expert squeeze work for you instead of against you? Here are some recommendations to consider:

1. *Match the problem you face with the most appropriate solution.* As we have seen throughout this chapter, the wide variety of decision-making problems requires a range of solutions. So consider carefully what kind of decision you are making and what approaches may be most helpful for you. What we know is that experts do a poor job in many settings, suggesting that you should try to supplement expert views with other approaches.

2. *Seek diversity.* Tetlock's work shows that while expert predictions are poor overall, some are better than others. What distinguishes predictive ability is not who the experts are or what they believe, but rather how they think. Borrowing from Archilochus—through Isaiah Berlin—Tetlock sorted experts into hedgehogs and foxes. Hedgehogs know one big thing and try to explain everything through that lens. Foxes tend to know a little about a lot of things and are not married to a single explanation for complex problems.

Tetlock finds that foxes are better predictors than hedge-hogs. Foxes arrive at their decisions by stitching "together diverse sources of information," lending credence to the importance of diversity. Naturally, hedgehogs are periodically right—and often spectacularly so—but do not predict as well as foxes over time.[29] For many important decisions, diversity is the key at both the individual and collective levels.

3. *Use technology when possible.* Offset the expert squeeze by leveraging technology, as Best Buy and Harrah's have. While growing, the list of organizations using computers and data to solve problems remains woeful.

Flooded with candidates and aware of the futility of most interviews, Google decided to create algorithms to identify attractive potential employees. First, the company asked seasoned employees to fill out a three-hundred-question survey, capturing details about their tenure, their behavior, and their personality. The company then compared the survey results to measures of employee performance, seeking connections. Among other findings, Google executives recognized that academic accomplishments did not always correlate with on-the-job performance. This novel approach enabled Google to sidestep problems with ineffective interviews and to start addressing the discrepancy.[30]

Sometimes organizations do not take advantage of information that is already available and relevant. A few years ago I was on a panel with the senior executive in charge of disaster services at the American Red Cross, the person who prepared for, and reacted to, national disasters. He told the amazing story of the relief efforts following Hurricane Katrina and mentioned other risks on the horizon. During my talk, I shared the probabilities of various disasters—the spread of avian flu, terrorist acts, hurricane frequencies—based on prices I had gleaned from a prediction market that morning.

My comments clearly intrigued the executive, who quickly approached me after the formal session. The disasters I discussed were precisely what he was paid to worry about, yet he could never judge their probability in real time. In this case, the missing component was simply awareness that the data was out there.

You could fill your shelves with books celebrating the wisdom of crowds, intuition, number crunching, or experts. But as a thoughtful decision maker, your prime task is to identify the nature of your problem and then consider how best to solve it. Since all approaches have pros and cons, there is no unique solution.

That said, the expert squeeze is real. Technology is enabling decision makers to gain valuable insights, and some organizations are moving toward new approaches to inform their decisions. But the biggest obstacle is the fundamental discomfort most of us have in handing over decisions previously made by experts to either computers or collectives. While the evidence against experts is in and clearly damning, human nature remains a high hurdle.

CHAPTER FOUR

Situational Awareness

How Accordian Music Boosts Sales of Burgundy

T ONY, A MIDDLE-AGED MAN with his glasses perched on the end of his nose, was the last to answer. He had a furrowed brow and appeared nervous. "Same," he replied without conviction. With that incorrect response, Tony added evidence to one of the most famous social psychology experiments—Solomon Asch's study of conformity under group pressure.

Asch first ran these experiments in the 1940s. He assembled a group of eight people. Unbeknownst to the true subject, seven of the participants were accomplices. Asch asked them to complete the trivial task of matching the length of a given line with one of three unequal lines. The procedure was simple, and the answers were virtually error-free in the control rounds. Asch then launched the experiment, cueing the confederates to give the wrong answer to see how the subject, who answered last, would respond. While some did remain independent, about one-third of the subjects conformed to the group's incorrect judgment.[1] The experiment showed that group decisions, even obviously poor ones, influence our individual decisions.

References to Asch's experiment are common, and most people who discuss it are satisfied to point out the degree of conformity. But the real question is: *what's going on in the heads of people who conform?* Asch wondered this, too. Based on close observation, he suggested three descriptive categories to explain the conforming behavior:

- *Distortion of judgment.* These subjects conclude that their perceptions are wrong and that the group is right.

- *Distortion of action.* These individuals suppress their own knowledge in order to go with the majority.

- *Distortion of perception.* This group is not aware that the majority opinion distorts their estimates.

Asch recognized that figuring out why people conform is as important as the observation that they do conform. But given the available tools, he had no concrete method for figuring out the mental processes behind conformity.

Fast forward five decades to the functional magnetic resonance imaging (fMRI) lab at Emory University. Gregory Berns, a neuroscientist, decided to run a variation of the Asch experiment with the ambitious goal of determining what is going on in the brains of the conforming individuals. Berns changed the task from matching lines to judging whether a three-dimensional figure was the same or different after a rotation period (see figure 4-1). While somewhat more difficult than Asch's task, subjects still got the right answer about nine out of ten times during control rounds. Similar to Asch, Berns found that even though some individuals stuck to their guns, about 40 percent conformed when the group presented the wrong answer.[2]

But Berns had something Asch could only dream of—an fMRI machine, which allowed him to put Asch's descriptive categories to the test by peering into the brains of the subjects. For distortions in judgment or action, you would expect activity in the forebrain, while distortions of perception would be in the posterior brain, regions controlling visual and spatial perception.

Contrary to what you might expect, for the conforming subjects, the scientists saw activity in the areas of the brain that work on mental rotation. This suggests that the group's choice affects the subject's *perception*. Equally surprising, the researchers did not find a meaningful change in activity in the frontal lobe, an area associated with the higher-order mental activities like judgment or action. Berns posits that the group's wrong answers impose a virtual image on the conformer's mind, eclipsing his or her own eyes. "We like to think that seeing is believing," said Berns, but "seeing is believing what the group tells you to believe."[3]

What happened to the people who remained independent when faced with the group's wrong responses? Those subjects experienced increased activity in the amygdala, a region that sends signals to prepare for immediate action. Fear is the amygdala's most effective trigger; the amygdala initiates the fight-or-flight response. So the brain activity of the subjects who remained independent suggests that while standing alone is commendable, it is unpleasant.[4]

Tony was a participant in a made-for-television study that Berns did for the ABC show *Primetime*. Berns recruited people off the

FIGURE 4-1

Variation of the Asch experiment—rotating 3-D objects

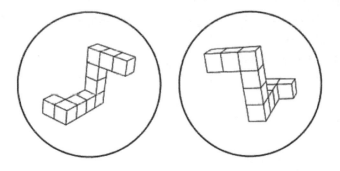

Source: Reprinted from *Biological Psychiatry*, Gregory S. Berns, Jonathan Chappelow, Caroline F. Zink, Giuseppe Pagnoni, Megan Martin-Skurski, and Jim Richards, "Neurobiological Correlates of Social Conformity and Independence During Mental Rotation," June 22, 2005, with permission from Society of Biological Psychiatry.

---

street, placed them into groups of six, and replicated the experiment with cameras rolling. Tony was the subject in his group. Before the experiment formally started he got the rotation task right 90 percent of the time, but dropped to a 10 percent accuracy rate in the face of the group's wrong answers. "You know, five people are seeing it and I'm not. I just went along with the answers," Tony said after the experiment. We now know why.[5]

Situation Trumps Disposition

The heart of this chapter's message is that our situation influences our decisions enormously. The mistakes that follow are particularly difficult to avoid because these influences are largely subconscious. Making good decisions in the face of subconscious pressure requires a very high degree of background knowledge and self-awareness.

How do you feel when you read the word "treasure"? Do you feel good? What images come to mind? If you are like most people, just ruminating on "treasure" gives you a little lift. Our minds naturally make connections and associate ideas. So if someone introduces a cue to you—a word, a smell, a symbol—your mind often starts down an associative path. And you can be sure the initial cue will color a decision that waits at the path's end. All this happens outside of your perception.[6]

People around us also influence our decisions, often with good reason. Social influence arises for a couple of reasons. The first is asymmetric information, a fancy phrase meaning someone knows something you don't. In those cases, imitation makes sense because the information upgrade allows you to make better decisions.

Peer pressure, or the desire to be part of the in-group, is a second source of social influence. For good evolutionary reasons, humans like to be part of a group—a collection of interdependent individuals—and naturally spend a good deal of time assessing who is "in" and who is "out."[7] Experiments in social psychology have repeatedly confirmed this. Researchers have done the Asch experiment over a hundred times in nearly twenty countries and have found similar conformity levels across geographies. Of course, conformity is also at the core of the diversity breakdowns that lead to unhealthy crowd behavior.

Lee Ross, a social psychologist at Stanford University, coined the term "fundamental attribution error" to describe the tendency to explain behavior based on an individual's disposition versus the situation. We naturally associate bad behavior with poor character, except when we assess our own behavior. We more readily explain our own poor behavior as a reflection of the social circumstances.[8]

Perhaps the most disconcerting aspect of situational power is that it can work for evil as well as for good. For people making important decisions, the negative aspect of the situation is especially worrisome. Some of the greatest atrocities known to mankind resulted from putting normal people into bad situations. While we all like to believe that our choices are largely independent of our circumstances, the evidence strongly suggests otherwise.

Most people, including psychologists, assume that decision-making mistakes apply universally across cultures and time. But research by Richard Nisbett, a psychologist at the University of Michigan, suggests important cultural differences exist between how Easterners and Westerners perceive the causes of behavior. Different economic, social, and philosophical traditions have shaped two distinct perceptions of social events. Easterners provide more situational explanations, while Westerners focus more on the individual. This leads to a host of potential cognitive differences, including patterns of attention (Easterners are attuned to environments and Westerners to objects), beliefs about the degree of control (Westerners believe that they are more in control), and assumptions about change (Easterners are more open to change).[9]

A study of how the media treated a pair of murder-suicide cases underscores the East-West cognitive gap. In the fall of 1991, a Chinese physics student lost an award competition, failed on appeal, and could not secure an academic post. He went to the physics department and shot his adviser, the person handling his appeal, and then himself. Two weeks later, an American postal worker lost his job, unsuccessfully appealed the dismissal, and could not find work. He stormed the post office and shot his supervisor, the individual who reviewed his appeal, and himself.

The researchers compared the treatment of the incidents in the press, including the *New York Times* (English) and the *World Journal* (Chinese), to see whether there were perceptual differences. They found that the Western press focused largely on the flaws and problems of the perpetrators ("very bad temper," "mentally unstable"), while the Eastern press emphasized the relationships and social context ("did not get along with his adviser," "influenced by the example of a recent mass slaying in Texas"). Follow-up queries of American and Chinese college students yielded identical perceptions. While all people are susceptible to the fundamental attribution error to some degree, the propensity is clearly different between Eastern and Western cultures.[10]

Some Wine with Your Music?

Imagine strolling down the supermarket aisle and coming upon a display of French and German wines, roughly matched for price and quality. You do some quick comparisons, place a German wine in your cart, and continue shopping. After you check out, a researcher approaches and asks why you bought the German wine. You mention the price, the wine's dryness, and how you anticipate it will go nicely with a meal you are planning. The researcher then asks whether you noticed the German music playing and whether it had any bearing on your decision. Like most, you would acknowledge hearing the music and avow that it had nothing to do with your selection.

This scenario is based on an actual study, and the results reveal the chapter's first mistake: belief that our decisions are independent of our experiences. In this test, the researchers placed the French and German wines next to each other, along with small national flags. Over two weeks, the scientists alternated playing

French accordion music and German Bierkeller pieces and watched
the results. When French music played, French wines represented
77 percent of the sales. When German music played, consumers
selected German wines 73 percent of the time. (See figure 4-2.) The
music made a huge difference in shaping purchases. But that's not
what the shoppers thought.

While the customers acknowledged that the music made them
think of either France or Germany, 86 percent denied the tunes had
any influence on their choice.[11] This experiment is an example of
priming, which psychologists formally define as "the incidental
activation of knowledge structures by the current situational context."[12] In other words, what comes in through our senses influences
how we make decisions, even when it seems completely irrelevant

FIGURE 4-2

Music subconsciously shaped purchase decisions

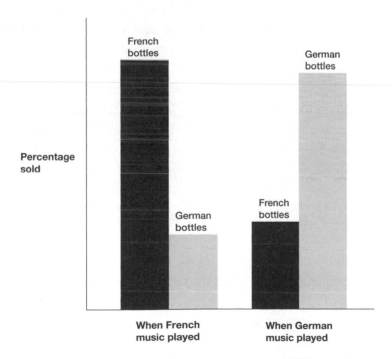

Source: Based on data from Adrian C. North, David J. Hargreaves, and Jennifer McKendrick, "In-store Music
Affects Product Choice," *Nature* 390 (November 13, 2007), 13.

in a logical sense. Priming is by no means limited to music. Researchers have manipulated behavior through exposure to words, smells, and visual backgrounds. For example, studies show:

- Immediately after being exposed to words associated with the elderly, primed subjects walked 13 percent slower than subjects seeing neutral words.[13]

- Exposure to the scent of an all-purpose cleaner prompted study participants to keep their environment tidier while eating a crumbly biscuit.[14]

- Subjects reviewing Web pages describing two sofa models preferred the more comfortable model when they saw a background with puffy clouds, and favored the cheaper sofa when they saw a background with coins.[15]

If you mention priming at a party, someone will inevitably raise subliminal advertising, such as flashing an advertisement for a soft-drink brand or food product prior to a movie to stimulate concession sales. This gimmick does not work because the connection between the prime and the subject's situational goals is generally too weak. While in your theater seat, your situational goal is to watch a film, not to select a soft-drink brand. For priming to work, the association must be sufficiently strong and the individual must be in a situation where the association sparks behavior.

The Fault of the Default

Are you in favor of organ donation? Have you consented to be an organ donor? If you are like most people, you answered yes to the first question. But the response to the second question depends a great deal on which country you live in. For instance, take neighboring countries Germany and Austria. Only 12 percent of Germans have explicitly consented to donate their organs, while virtually 100 percent of Austrians have offered presumed consent. (See figure 4-3.)

The difference? In Germany, you must opt in to become a donor. In Austria, you must opt out to avoid being a donor. The consent gap has less to do with attitudes about donating than it does with default options. The difference translates into saved lives; the actual rate of organ donation is notably higher in opt-out countries.[16]

The donor statistics point to our second mistake: the perception that people decide what is best for them independent of how the choice is framed. In reality, many people simply go with default options. This applies to a wide array of choices, from insignificant issues like the ringtone on a new cell phone to consequential issues like financial savings, educational choice, and medical alternatives.

FIGURE 4-3

How opt-in and opt-out policies shape consent rates

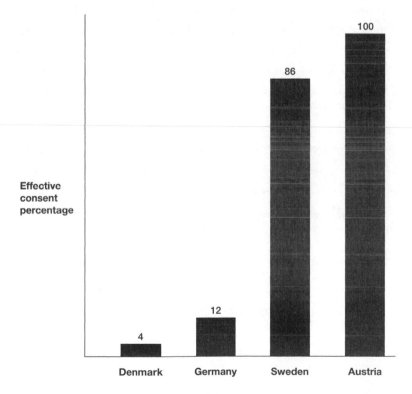

Source: Based on data from Eric J. Johnson and Daniel Goldstein, "Do Defaults Save Lives?" *Science* 302 (November 21, 2003), 1338–1339.

Richard Thaler, an economist, and Cass Sunstein, a law professor, call the relationship between choice presentation and the ultimate decision "choice architecture." They convincingly argue that we can easily nudge people toward a particular decision based solely on how we arrange the choices for them.[17]

People who structure choices create a context for decision making. Since many people go with the default alternatives, choice architects can influence the quality of decisions for large groups, for better or for worse. Thaler and Sunstein advocate for an idea they call "libertarian paternalism," where the default is a good choice for many (paternalism), yet individuals can depart from the default if they want to (libertarianism). Choice architects—doctors, businesspeople, government officials—are everywhere and operate with a wide range of skill and awareness.

A prominent psychologist who is popular on the speaker circuit told me a story that underscores how underappreciated choice architecture remains. When companies call to invite him to speak, he offers them two choices. Either they can pay him his set fee and get a standard presentation, or they can pay him nothing in exchange for the opportunity to work with him on an experiment to improve choice architecture (e.g., redesign a form or Web site). Of course, the psychologist benefits by getting more real-world results on choice architecture, but it seems like a pretty good deal for the company as well, because an improved architecture might translate into financial benefits vastly in excess of his speaking fee. He noted ruefully that so far not one company has taken him up on his experiment offer.

I Like X, Therefore I Decide in Favor of X

Do you know anyone who routinely buys insurance *and* plays the lottery? If so, you can describe your acquaintance as both a normal human and someone who violates the principles of expected utility. The buyer of insurance and lottery tickets also personifies a third mistake: relying on immediate emotional reactions to risk instead of on an impartial judgment of possible future outcomes.[18] Using the distinction between System 1 (the fast, experiential one) and System 2 (the slower, analytical one), this mistake arises when the experiential system overrides the analytical system, leading to decisions that deviate substantially from the ideal.

The central idea is called *affect,* or how the positive or negative emotional impression of a stimulus influences decisions. The basic concept is that how we feel about something influences how we decide about it. Affective responses occur quickly and automatically, are difficult to manage, and remain beyond our awareness. As Robert Zajonc, a social psychologist, said, "In many decisions affect plays a more important role than we are willing to admit. We sometimes delude ourselves that we proceed in a rational manner and weigh all the pros and cons of the various alternatives. But this is probably seldom the case. Quite often 'I decided in favor of X' is no more than 'I liked X.'"[19] Affect is situational because it often follows vivid outcomes or a specific individual experience.[20]

Affect research reveals two core principles related to probabilities and outcomes. First, when the outcomes of an opportunity are without potent affective meaning, people tend to overweight probabilities. As a case in point, Paul Slovic, a psychology professor at the University of Oregon, asked one group to rate a system to save 150 lives and a separate group to rate a system expected to save 98 percent of 150 lives. Even though saving 150 lives is clearly better, the 98 percent option received a much higher rating. The reason is that the first group found little affective value in the 150 sum. On the other hand, 98 percent, close to the ideal of 100 percent, was affectively stronger. Therefore, the probability took center stage in the rating.[21]

In contrast, when outcomes are vivid, people pay too little attention to the probabilities and too much to the outcomes. For example, lottery players have the same feeling whether the probability of winning is one in ten million or one in ten thousand because the payoff is so large and carries so much affective meaning. This probability insensitivity is why individuals simultaneously play the lottery and buy insurance: the valence of the lottery gains or property losses swamps the associated probabilities of winning or losing.

Becoming Your Role

"Ordinary people, simply doing their jobs, and without any particular hostility on their part, can become agents in a terrible destructive process," wrote Stanley Milgram.[22] His comment summarizes the core lesson from his well-known study of obedience to authority. Milgram, a psychologist who studied under Asch, showed that under certain conditions, subjects would yield to authority and deliver lethal shocks to punish another experiment participant. Of course, the shocks were fake—even though the subjects did not know that—but under the authoritarian watch of the experiment supervisor, most individuals obediently inflicted astounding amounts of pain. The subjects administered shocks at higher levels than various groups had predicted prior to the experiments, and roughly half the participants continued to the maximum shock level (ominously labeled *xxx* on the shock generator). Jerry Burger, a psychologist at Santa Clara University, recently completed a modified version of the experiment with results similar to those of Milgram nearly a half-century earlier.[23]

Milgram's experiment draws out this chapter's final mistake: explaining behavior by focusing on people's dispositions, rather than considering the situation. This is a restatement of the fundamental attribution error. The vital point is that the situation is generally much more powerful than most people—especially Westerners—acknowledge. The combination of the sense of group and the setting lays the groundwork for behavior that can deviate substantially from the norm.

Philip Zimbardo, a psychologist at Stanford University, did an experiment in 1971 that ranks with Asch and Milgram in exhibiting the power of the situation. To start, Zimbardo advertised for volunteers in a two-week-long prison experiment, offering $15 a day. He ran the seventy applicants through psychological and physical tests and ended up with twenty-four healthy, mentally stable, middle-class, male students from the Palo Alto, California, area.

By a flip of a coin, Zimbardo assigned half the volunteers to be prisoners and the rest to be prison guards. One morning, a Palo Alto police car picked up the prisoners, "charging" them with armed robbery and burglary. The guards were assigned to work one of three eight-hour shifts.

With the help of prison consultants, Zimbardo built a prison in the basement of the building that housed Stanford's psychology department. On arrival at the jail, the guards and warden took steps to humiliate, dehumanize, and oppress the prisoners.

Although Zimbardo randomly designated the roles, the situation clearly shaped behavior. He noticed that the volunteers (and he himself) started to act out their assigned roles. The prisoners tried various tactics to gain advantage over the guards and tried to escape, while the guards schemed to keep the prisoners in check. Concerned that the guards were heaping too much abuse on the prisoners, Zimbardo questioned the situation's morality and ended the study after only five days.[24]

Zimbardo explains the factors that make the situation so forceful. First, situational power is most likely in novel settings, where there are no previous behavioral guidelines. Second, rules—which may emerge through interaction or be predetermined—can create a means to dominate and suppress others because people justify their behavior as only conforming to the rules. Third, when people are asked to play a certain role for a prolonged period, they risk becoming actors who can't break from character. Roles shut people off from their normal lives and accommodate behaviors they would generally avoid. Finally, in situations that lead to negative behavior, there is often an enemy—an outside group. This is especially pronounced when both the in-group and out-group stop focusing on individuals.[25]

Zimbardo ends *The Lucifer Effect*, his book on situational power, on an encouraging note, offering tips for resisting the pull of unwelcome social influence. At their core, most of the recommendations have the same message: be mindful of what is going on around you.

The Power of Inertia

Inertia, or resistance to change, also shows how the situation shapes real-world decisions. A common answer to "Why do we do it this way?" is "We've always done it this way." Individuals and organizations perpetuate poor practices even when their original usefulness has disappeared or better methods have surfaced. The situation keeps people from taking a fresh look at old problems.

In 1990, when David Johnson took over as chief executive officer, the Campbell Soup Company substantially lagged its peers in financial measures like return on equity and earnings growth. Johnson was keen to consider any operational changes that would allow for better returns and growth. In reviewing operations, he noticed an annual autumn promotion of tomato soup, the company's highly profitable flagship product. Suspecting the campaign was a waste of money, Johnson asked why the program existed. The executive in charge replied, "I don't know. To the best of my knowledge, we've always had a fall promotion."

Johnson did more research. Around the time of World War I, Campbell decided to grow its own produce to assure its quality. In the eight weeks of the tomato harvest, the company dedicated all its capacity to producing tomato soup and juice. At the end of the harvest, Campbell's inventory was up to the rafters, while the heart of the soup season still lay months ahead. So the company started running a promotion to move the inventory.

Naturally, in the eighty years between the original decision and Johnson's investigation, the company had advanced to finding sources for tomatoes throughout the year, thereby avoiding a bulge in seasonal inventory and eliminating the need for the promotion. But the fall promotion remained, an uneconomic vestige of quainter times. To overcome inertia, Peter Drucker, the legendary consultant, suggested asking the seemingly naïve question, "If we did not do this already, would we, knowing what we now know, go into it?"[26]

Regulations can result in another form of inertia. Most people (including doctors) think of medicine as a craft, in which doctors diagnose and treat patients according to their needs. Creating rigid procedures, like a pilot's checklist, feels overly restrictive. Yet using checklists can help doctors save lives. It's not that the doctors don't know what to do—for the most part, they know their stuff—it's just they don't always follow all the steps they should. When asked why doctors generally shun checklists, Joseph Britto, a former doctor, quipped, "Unlike pilots, doctors don't go down with their planes."[27]

Dr. Atul Gawande, a surgeon and writer, explained how regulatory inertia trumped good decision making, even when the consequence was a matter of life and death.[28] Gawande told of Dr. Peter Pronovost, an anesthesiologist and critical-care specialist at the Johns Hopkins Hospital. The death of his father because of a medical error encouraged Pronovost to dedicate his career to ensuring the safety of patients. He started modestly with a five-step checklist to help prevent infections as the result of inserting large intravenous lines into patients. In the United States, medical professionals put roughly 5 million lines into patients each year, and about 4 percent of those patients become infected within a week and a half. The added cost of treating those patients is roughly $3 billion per year, and the complications result in twenty to thirty thousand annual preventable deaths.

There was nothing revolutionary about Pronovost's checklist, which reflected the standard steps that doctors had been taught for years. Even so, he observed that the physicians skipped at least one step for about one-third of the patients, generally because they were too busy attending to more-pressing issues. So he persuaded the hospital administrators to have the nurses make sure that the doctors followed all the steps. When slipping off course, the doctors would have a nurse to nudge them back.

Pronovost began the program at the Johns Hopkins Hospital, where the rate of infections plummeted. The hospital administrators estimated that using the checklist for this single procedure saved numerous lives and millions of dollars in the first few years.

Encouraged by these results, Pronovost convinced the Michigan Health & Hospital Association to adopt his checklists. The rate of infection in that state was above the national average. But after using the checklists for just three months, it had dropped by two-thirds. The program saved an estimated fifteen hundred lives and nearly $200 million in the first eighteen months.

Pronovost's work did not go unnoticed. Other states began to consider the program, *Time* magazine named him one of the one hundred most influential people in the world, and he received a prestigious MacArthur "genius" grant.

But then inertia got in the way.

Toward the end of 2007, a federal agency called the Office for Human Research Protections charged that the Michigan program violated federal regulations. Its baffling rationale was that the checklist represented an alteration in medical care similar to an experimental drug and should continue only with federal monitoring and the explicit written approval of the patient. While the agency eventually allowed the work to continue, concerns about federal regulations needlessly delayed the program's progress elsewhere in the United States. Bureaucratic inertia triumphed over a better approach.

Here are some ideas to help you cope with the power of the situation:

1. *Be aware of your situation.* You can think of this in two parts. There is the conscious element, where you can create

a positive environment for decision making in your own surroundings by focusing on process, keeping stress to an acceptable level, being a thoughtful choice architect, and making sure to diffuse the forces that encourage negative behaviors.

Then there is coping with the subconscious influences. Control over these influences requires awareness of the influence, motivation to deal with it, and the willingness to devote attention to address possible poor decisions. In the real world, satisfying all three control conditions is extremely difficult, but the path starts with awareness.[29]

2. *Consider the situation first and the individual second.* This concept, called attributional charity, insists that you evaluate the decisions of others by starting with the situation and then turning to the individuals, not the other way around. While easier for Easterners than Westerners, most of us consistently underestimate the role of the situation in assessing the decisions we see others make. Try not to make the fundamental attribution error.[30]

3. *Watch out for the institutional imperative.* Warren Buffett, the celebrated investor and chairman of Berkshire Hathaway, coined the term *institutional imperative* to explain the tendency of organizations to "mindlessly" imitate what peers are doing. There are typically two underlying drivers of the imperative. First, companies want to be part of the in-group, much as individuals do. So if some companies in an industry are doing mergers, chasing growth, or expanding geographically, others will be tempted to follow. Second are incentives. Executives often reap financial rewards by following the group. When decision makers make money from being part of the crowd, the draw is nearly inescapable.[31]

One example comes from a *Financial Times* interview with the former chief executive officer of Citigroup Chuck

Prince in 2007, before the brunt of the financial crisis. "When the music stops, things will be complicated," offered Prince, demonstrating that he had some sense of what was to come. "But as long as the music is playing, you've got to get up and dance."[32] The institutional imperative is rarely a good dance partner.

4. *Avoid inertia.* Periodically revisit your processes and ask whether they are serving their purpose. Organizations sometimes adopt routines and structures that become crystallized, impeding positive change. Efforts to reform education in the United States, for example, have been met with resistance from teachers and administrators who prefer the status quo.

We like to think of ourselves as good decision makers; we weigh the facts, consider the alternatives, and select the best course of action. We perceive ourselves as largely immune to the influence of others as we decide and act. We convince ourselves that the facts and our experience carry the day, not the behavioral vagaries of those around us.

Unfortunately, reality flatly contradicts our perceptions. Decision making, whether in the medical office, the boardroom, or the courtroom, is an inherently social exercise. Primes, defaults, affect, and the behaviors of those around us weigh on how we decide and frequently in ways that are beyond our consciousness. A thoughtful decision maker recognizes these myriad influences and works to successfully manage them.

CHAPTER FIVE

More Is Different

How Bees Find the Best Hive Without a Real Estate Agent

I F YOU WATCH AN ANT try to accomplish something, you'll be impressed by how inept it is," says Deborah Gordon, a biologist at Stanford University who studies ant behavior. But she adds quickly, "Ants aren't smart, ant colonies are."[1] Social insects like ants, bees, and termites are among nature's most wondrous creatures. Colonies of these seemingly simple species have flourished for tens of millions of years without anyone in charge. The colonies successfully feed, fight, and reproduce, with each insect following simple rules, acting on local information, and remaining clueless about what's going on in the colony as a whole.

Humans are more hierarchical and habitually rely on specialists. For instance, how did you find your current home? You probably found a real estate agent who showed you location after location until you identified one that was geographically suitable, the right size, and within your price range. Using synoptic knowledge of the market and your needs, the broker matched you with an appropriate seller.

So how would you find an appropriate home for thousands of individuals?

Honey bees have solved this problem. As late spring approaches, the queen and roughly half of a thriving hive leave to start a new colony. Almost ten thousand strong, the swarm first stops at a nearby tree branch where the bees form a beardlike cluster. Eventually, they take off together for their new home, usually a desirable hollow tree in the distance.

Beekeepers observed this swarming process for centuries without understanding how the bees do it. To answer that question, Thomas Seeley and Kirk Visscher, biologists who specialize in understanding bee behavior, set up controlled conditions and carefully studied how the swarm found a new home. The scientists brought swarms of bees, each bee marked for identification, to an isolated island off the coast of Maine. They then set up five boxes for the bees to choose from, including a dream bee abode with the ideal size, height, and orientation. The island is nearly treeless, which limited the real estate market and assured that the bees would select among the boxes of varying attractiveness.

Seeley and Visscher found that only a few hundred bees go out to scout and appraise their options. Upon returning to the swarm, any scout bee that has found an attractive possible home does a waggle dance, a number of circuits in a figure-eight pattern, with the angle of the dance indicating location and the duration reflecting the site's quality. The better the site, the longer the dance.

So far, so good. But here's what surprised the scientists: the decision to take off to a new home does not happen at the bee bivouac, as you might expect if you have a wisdom-of-crowds mind-set. Rather, the bees make the choice at the prospective nest site. Once the scouts see about fifteen other scouting bees near a possible home, they sense a quorum. They then fly back to the swarm, stimulate it into flight, and guide the group to their new dwelling. As Seeley recaps, "It's a race among possible sites to gain support. Which site first builds to 15 bees wins." Remarkably, the bees almost always pick the best site.[2]

Swarms have much to teach us, from running a committee meeting to solving difficult combinatorial problems.[3] But to introduce this chapter's decision-making mistake, I want to focus on why swarm intelligence is so counterintuitive: you cannot understand the swarm's complex behavior by analyzing the decisions of a few key individuals. Unlike most human institutions, there is no leader. It is a world free of budgets, strategic plans, and deadlines, so you can't surmise why the group is so effective by interviewing its individual members.

In fact, Seeley and Visscher found that the signal of any individual scout bee was "extremely noisy" and that only the aggregation of the individuals allowed the group to figure out what to do.[4] We cannot understand, let alone manage, a complex adaptive system at the wrong level. Yet the tendency to interpret the behavior of a complex system from its components is as common as it is wrong.

Complex Adaptive Systems—The Whole Is Smarter Than Its Parts

Let's define a complex adaptive system and explain why it flummoxes observers. You can think of a complex adaptive system in three parts (see figure 5-1).[5] First, there is a group of heterogeneous

FIGURE 5-1

Simple description of a complex adaptive system

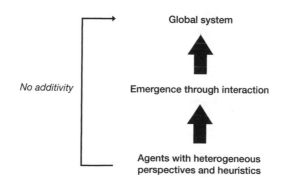

agents. These agents can be neurons in your brain, bees in a hive, investors in a market, or people in a city. Heterogeneity means each agent has different and evolving decision rules that both reflect the environment and attempt to anticipate change in it. Second, these agents interact with one another, and their interactions create structure—scientists often call this *emergence*. Finally, the structure that emerges behaves like a higher-level system and has properties and characteristics that are distinct from those of the underlying agents themselves.

Think of Deborah Gordon's comments. Even though the individual ants are inept, the colony as a whole is smart. The whole is greater than the sum of the parts. The inability to understand the system based on its components prompted Philip Anderson, a physicist and Nobel Prize winner, to draft the essay, "More Is Different." Anderson wrote, "The behavior of large and complex aggregates of elementary particles, it turns out, is not to be understood in terms of the simple extrapolation of the properties of a few particles. Instead, at each level of complexity entirely new properties appear."[6] If you want to understand an ant colony, don't ask an ant. It doesn't know what's going on. Study the colony.

The problem goes beyond the inscrutable nature of complex adaptive systems. Humans have a deep desire to understand cause and effect, as such links probably conferred humans with evolutionary advantage.[7] In complex adaptive systems, there is no simple method for understanding the whole by studying the parts, so searching for simple agent-level causes of system-level effects is useless. Yet our minds are not beyond making up a cause to relieve the itch of an unexplained effect.[8] When a mind seeking links between cause and effect meets a system that conceals them, accidents will happen.

The first mistake, inappropriately extrapolating individual behavior to explain collective behavior, is one I ran into early in my career. From the moment I started on Wall Street, I heard that a company's earnings per share are the key to its stock price. Investors, executives, and the media still beat that drum. But I then saw studies by financial economists who concluded that cash flow drove stock prices, not earnings.[9] So, which is it?

It turns out the earnings and cash flow camps addressed the question using two very different approaches. The earnings camp listens to what people talk about day-to-day, including the investment community's chatter, what hits CNBC's screens, and the stories on the *Wall Street Journal's* pages. In contrast, the economists look at how the *market* behaves. One group focuses on the components, the other on the aggregate. Research in experimental economics, for example, shows that markets can generate very efficient prices even when the individual participants have limited information. Just as watching one bee won't help you understand the hive's behavior, listening to individual investors will give you scant insight into the market.[10]

I have explained to executives countless times that the opinion of the market is far more relevant than the utterances of individuals. By studying the market, we can get a much better sense of how various decisions affect economic value than we can by listening to partially informed individuals. This is not just an issue of academic interest: a recent survey of executives showed that 80 percent of them would forgo value-creating investments to meet an earnings target.[11]

That misplaced emphasis is crucial for executives, who rely more on the dubious guidance of highly compensated advisers—who get paid to do deals—than on the collective wisdom of the market. The mental shift from the individual to the collective is difficult, especially because individual opinions are much more accessible and persuasive.[12]

Regrettably, this mistake also shows up in behavioral finance, a field that considers the role of psychology in economic decision making. Behavioral finance enthusiasts believe that since individuals are irrational—counter to classical economic theory—and markets are made up of individuals, then markets must be irrational. This is like saying, "We have studied ants and can show that they are bumbling and inept. Therefore, we can reason that ant colonies are bumbling and inept." But that conclusion doesn't hold if more is different—and it is. Market irrationality *does not* follow from individual irrationality. You and I both might be irrationally over-confident, for example, but if you are an overconfident buyer and I am an overconfident seller, our biases may cancel out. In dealing with systems, the collective behavior matters more. You must care-fully consider the unit of analysis to make a proper decision.

Unintended Consequences: Feed an Elk, Starve an Ecosystem

When you are dealing with a system that has lots of interconnected parts, tweaking one part can have unforeseen consequences for the whole. Take the example of Yellowstone National Park. In retro-spect, it looks like the park's woes started when explorers in the mid-1800s couldn't find enough food in large areas of its 2.2 million acres. Formally designated in 1872, Yellowstone had seen much of its game—elk, bison, antelope, deer—disappear at the hands of hunters and poachers in the preceding decades. So in 1886, the United States Cavalry was called in to run the park. One of its first orders of business was to resuscitate the park's game population.

After a few years of special feeding and favorable treatment, the elk population swelled rapidly. Indeed, the animals became so abun-dant they started overgrazing, depleting essential flora and causing soil erosion. From there, events cascaded: The decline in aspen trees, consumed by the hungry elk, shrunk the beaver population. The dams the beavers built were important to the ecosystem because they slowed the spring runoff from streams, discouraged erosion, and kept the water clean so that trout could spawn. Without the beavers, the ecosystem deteriorated rapidly.

Yet the managers of the park were oblivious to the fact that the elk population explosion was responsible for the trouble. Indeed, after roughly 60 percent of the elk population starved to death or succumbed to disease in the winter of 1919–1920, the National Park

Service overlooked the lack of food and falsely blamed the deaths on another group of Yellowstone residents: the predators.

Taking the situation into their own hands, they killed (often illegally and illicitly) wolves, mountain lions, and coyotes. Yet the more they killed, the worse the situation grew. The population of game animals began to experience erratic booms and busts. This only encouraged the managers to redouble their efforts, triggering a morbid feedback loop. By the mid-1900s, they had all but eliminated the predators. For example, the National Park Service shot the last of the wolves in 1926, only to reintroduce them roughly seventy years later.[13]

And so it went. The bungling supervision of Yellowstone illustrates a second mistake that surrounds complex systems: how addressing one component of the system can have unintended consequences for the whole. Alston Chase wrote about the National Park Service, "They had been playing God for ninety-five years and everything they did seemed to make the park worse. In their attempts to manage this beautiful wild area, they seemed caught in a terrible ratchet, where each mistake made the park worse off and no mistake could be corrected."[14]

That unintended system-level consequences arise from even the best-intentioned individual-level actions has long been recognized.[15] But the decision-making challenge remains for a couple of reasons. First, our modern world has more interconnected systems than before. So we encounter these systems with greater frequency and, most likely, with greater consequence. Second, we still attempt to cure problems in complex systems with a naïve understanding of cause and effect.

The U.S. Government's decision to allow Lehman Brothers, the investment bank, to fail in September 2008 is a good illustration. The government's position was that since the market largely understood Lehman's poor financial condition, it could absorb the consequences. But the bankruptcy announcement roiled global financial markets because Lehman's losses were larger than people thought initially, contributing to an increase in global risk aversion. Even parts of the market that were perceived to be safe, like money market funds, received a jolt. For example, the Reserve Primary Fund, one of the oldest and largest money market mutual funds in the United States, announced it had lost money for its fund holders because the Lehman Brothers debt that it held had been wiped out. The announcement shocked investors and undermined confidence in the broader financial system.[16]

This challenge spills over into other fields as well. For example, Murray Bowen, a psychiatrist at Georgetown University, recognized this problem in his study and treatment of schizophrenic patients.[17] Early in his career as a doctor, Bowen's study of a wide range of disciplines convinced him to take a broader view of mental health than was common at the time. While the standard treatment focused exclusively on the individual, Bowen saw the patient in the context of a family system. Accordingly, Bowen Theory offers approaches to understanding and treating individual behaviors as part of an interconnected family and social system. We can easily see how similar issues arise in Western medicine, where incentives have led to more specialists (the parts) at the expense of primary care physicians (the whole).[18]

The Constellation Matters More Than Its Brightest Star

What is the quickest way to improve your organization's results? Many companies, sports teams, and entertainment businesses opt for the same solution: they hire a star. At first glance, signing a star seems like a great idea because of the promise of a quick performance boost. More often than not, however, stars fail to live up to expectations in their new roles.[19] One explanation lies in our next systems-related mistake, isolating individual performance without proper consideration of the individual's surrounding system.

To be clear, reversion to the mean probably accounts for some part of a star's fading performance. But that's not the whole story. A star's performance relies to some degree on the people, structure, and norms around him—the system. Analyzing results requires sorting the relative contributions of the individual versus the system, something we are not particularly good at. When we err, we tend to overstate the role of the individual.

This mistake is consequential because organizations routinely pay big bucks to lure high performers, only to be sorely disappointed. In one study, a trio of professors from Harvard Business School tracked more than one thousand acclaimed equity analysts over a decade and monitored how their performance changed as they switched firms. Their dour conclusion, "When a company hires a star, the star's performance plunges, there is a sharp decline in the functioning of the group or team the person works with, and the company's market value falls."[20] The hiring organization is let down because it failed to consider systems-based advantages that the prior employer supplied, including firm reputation and resources. Employers also underestimate the relationships that supported previous success, the quality of the other employees, and a familiarity with past processes.

All three mistakes have the same root: a focus on an isolated part of a complex adaptive system without an appreciation of the system dynamics. Given the fact that technological, social, and environmental changes are accelerating, you can be sure that you will encounter complex systems with increasing frequency.

What should you do when you find yourself dealing with a complex adaptive system? Here are some thoughts that may help your decision making:

1. *Consider the system at the correct level.* Remember the phrase "more is different." The most prevalent trap is extrapolating the behavior of individual agents to gain a sense of system behavior. If you want to understand the stock market, study it at the market level. Consider what you see and read from individuals as entertainment, not as education. Similarly, be aware that the function of an individual agent outside the system may be very different from that

function within the system. For instance, mammalian cells have the same metabolic rates in vitro, whether they are from shrews or elephants. But the metabolic rate of cells in small mammals is much higher than the rate of those in large mammals. The same structural cells work at different rates, depending on the animals they find themselves in.[21]

2. *Watch for tightly coupled systems.* A system is tightly coupled when there is no slack between items, allowing a process to go from one stage to the next without any opportunity to intervene. Aircraft, space missions, and nuclear power plants are classic examples of complex, tightly coupled systems. Engineers try to build in buffers or redundancies to avoid failure, but frequently don't anticipate all possible contingencies.[22] Most complex adaptive systems are loosely coupled, where removing or incapacitating one or a few agents has little impact on the system's performance. For example, if you randomly remove some investors, the stock market will continue to function fine. But when the agents lose diversity and behave in a coordinated fashion, a complex adaptive system can behave in a tightly coupled fashion. Booms and crashes in financial markets are an illustration.

3. *Use simulations to create virtual worlds.* Dealing with complex systems is inherently tricky because the feedback is equivocal, information is limited, and there is no clear link between cause and effect. Simulation is a tool that can help our learning process. Simulations are low cost, provide feedback, and have proved their value in other domains like military planning and pilot training.[23]

   Perhaps the best-known example for business is "The Beer Game," popularized by John Sterman, a management professor at MIT Sloan School of Management and the director of the MIT System Dynamics Group. The game's board portrays the beer value chain, and the instructor assigns the participants roles as retailers, wholesalers, distributors, or producers. Each simulated week, customers purchase beer, and the four teams within the value chain attempt to minimize their inventory and backlog costs, while trying to make sure they have enough stock for their customers. After thirty-six weeks, the team with the lowest costs wins.

Each team has good information about their inventory, backlog, and orders, but very limited information about what's going on for the game as a whole. Like Seeley's bees, each team has good local information but poor global information.

While the game has a relatively straightforward set-up, Sterman reports that the players struggle to comprehend the system and tend to make common mistakes. Orders and inventories fluctuate wildly, and the players often feel frustrated and helpless. Most players fail to understand how their individual decisions affect the system in the aggregate.

Having observed the game's results over time, Sterman writes, "Understanding how well intentioned, intelligent people can create an outcome that no one expected and no one wants is one of the profound lessons of the game."[24] Unfortunately, few individuals, organizations, or businesses use simulations, despite the lessons they offer.

"Orderly processes in creating human judgment and intuition lead people to wrong decisions when faced with complex and highly interacting systems," wrote Jay Forrester, the father of systems dynamics, nearly forty years ago.[25] Even though complex adaptive systems surround us more now, our minds are no more adept at understanding them. Our innate desire to grasp cause and effect leads us to understand the system at the wrong level, resulting in predictable mistakes. Complex adaptive systems often perform well at the system level, despite dumb agents (a point that both scientists and nonscientists often fail to grasp).[26] Conversely, unintended consequences can lead to failure when well-meaning individuals attempt to manage the system to achieve a particular goal. So if you deal with a complex adaptive system, make sure you carefully set your system-level goal and proceed with caution in implementing agent-level changes for achieving your objective.

CHAPTER SIX

Evidence of Circumstance

How Outsourcing the Dreamliner Became

Boeing's Nightmare

I F YOU ARE AN ADULT who was born in North America, there is about an 80 percent chance that you have one or more siblings. In considering the issues of family dynamics, few get as much attention as birth order. Firstborn children are perceived as serious, conscientious keepers of tradition, while later-born children have a more go-with-the-flow, adventurous attitude. And everybody knows that the youngest child gets away with everything. Birth order is clearly important within families.

In his 1996 book, *Born to Rebel*, Frank Sulloway extended birth-order dynamics into a sweeping new theory, arguing that birth order plays an important role in shaping personality. He posits that the children in a family seek alternative strategies to distinguish themselves, depending on the order in which they were born. Firstborns are generally ambitious, close minded, and conventional, while later-born children are venturesome, agreeable, and open minded (i.e., born to rebel).[1] His research suggests that people who are born later often come up with and accept new ideas, while firstborns stick with promoting and defending the status quo.

He claims that political and scientific revolutions are most likely led by later-borns and that firstborns often seek to quash new ideas. In full disclosure, I am a later-born.

Prominent scientists and critics initially received Sulloway's work approvingly, and the book sold well. But then a firestorm broke out. After reviewing Sulloway's methods and conclusions, a group challenged that the work did not hold up to scientific scrutiny.[2] Indeed, one of Sulloway's sources said he could "neither reconstruct nor understand" Sulloway's analysis.[3] Dalton Conley, a sociologist at New York University and a family dynamics expert, sniffed, "I don't think [Sulloway's] methodological means hold up at all. He does something you're not supposed to do in the social sciences, which is selectively choose the evidence that bolsters your arguments."[4] Sulloway remains unbowed, claiming his detractors do not understand his theory. In contemplating both sides of this debate, I am firmly in the camp that finds Sulloway's analysis and conclusions wanting.

"But wait," you are probably thinking, "I can attest from personal experience that birth order does matter. My bossy older sibling and/or irritating younger sibling were no figment of my imagination!" And you would be right. Birth order effects *do* exist within a family and they *do* shape behavior. Older children alternate between dominating and nurturing their younger siblings, acting like proxies for parents. Younger children get relatively more parental attention and affection.

So how can we at once accept that birth-order effects are real, while doubting Sulloway's claims? The answer lies in considering context.

While children assume birth-order roles within the family, they do not extend the roles outside the family. For instance, an oldest child who is domineering at home may show no such behavior on the playground at school. When parents or siblings complete self-report tests or assess a family member, birth-order effects show up clearly. But when outsiders like teachers or researchers observe behaviors, the birth-order effects melt away. Children—indeed people of all ages—do not behave the same under all conditions. They adjust their behavior to reflect their social circumstances.

Just a couple of months after our youngest child started preschool, my wife and I got a potentially disturbing call from his teachers. They were worried about his verbal development because he barely uttered a word at school. The good news was that he followed his lessons and activities fine; the bad news was that he did not make a peep.

My wife and I were less concerned than baffled. He is our fifth child and was from an early age the most verbal of the bunch—no doubt partly reflecting his personality and partly from coping with four older siblings. At home he was anything but quiet, but once he stepped into the classroom he turned off the verbal spigot. Fortunately, one of the teachers who had seen him at home assured the others that yes, the kid can talk, and talk plenty.

Where Sulloway overreached was in arguing that behaviors at home shape behaviors everywhere. The facts simply do not stand behind this assertion. More specifically, studies consistently show that birth order has little or no effect on personality. Cécile Ernst and Jules Angst, Swiss psychologists, did the most comprehensive study of birth order and personality and concluded flatly that birth order and family size do not have a strong impact on personality. In a more recent paper, "Rebel Without a Cause or Effect: Birth Order and Social Attitudes," a trio of sociologists found little or no support for Sulloway's claims.[5]

The lesson from this debate is an example of this chapter's theme: the importance of understanding context. Frequently, people try to cram the lessons or experiences from one situation into a different situation. But that strategy often crashes because the decisions that work in one context often fail miserably in another. The right answer to most questions that professionals face is, "It depends."

The Theory of Theory Building

Whether or not they are aware of it, people ground their choices in theory—a belief that a certain action will lead to a satisfactory outcome. Most professionals are wary of the word *theory* because they associate it with something that is impractical. But if you define theory as an explanation of cause and effect, it is eminently practical. Sound theory helps to predict how certain decisions lead to outcomes across a range of circumstances.

Paul Carlile and Clayton Christensen, both professors of management, describe the process of theory building in three stages.[6]

- The first stage is observation, which includes carefully measuring a phenomenon and documenting the results. The goal is to set common standards so that subsequent researchers can agree on the subject and the terms to describe it.

- The second stage is classification, where researchers simplify and organize the world into categories to clarify differences among phenomena. Early in theory development, these categories are based predominantly on attributes.

- The final stage is definition, or describing the relationship between the categories and the outcomes. Often, these relationships start as simple correlations.

Theories improve when researchers test predictions against real-world data, identify anomalies, and subsequently reshape the theory. Two crucial improvements occur during this refining process. In the classification stage, researchers evolve the categories to reflect circumstances, not just attributes. In other words, the categories go beyond what works to when it works. In the definition stage, the theory advances beyond simple correlations and sharpens to define causes—why it works. This pair of improvements allows people to go beyond crude attributes and to tailor their choices to the situation they face.

Carlile and Christensen offer the history of manned flight as an example. Early on, hopeful fliers studied animals that could fly and noticed they almost all had wings and feathers (observation and classification stages). There were some outliers, like ostriches and bats, but the correlation between feathered wings and flight was extremely high (definition stage). So early aviators fashioned wings, attached feathers, climbed up high, jumped, flapped, and crashed. The crash was an anomaly that forced the theory builders back to the drawing board.

In the 1700s, Daniel Bernoulli's study of fluid dynamics led to the airfoil, a shape that creates lift by creating decreased air pressure over the top of the wing relative to the air pressure under the wing. Rather than being correlated with flight, Bernoulli's Principle shows what causes flight (improved classification and definition stages). The airfoil led to a new approach to flying. Once the Wright brothers combined this new theory with the physical materials and capabilities of stability, steering, and propulsion, the era of flight was born.

Many management theories today look a lot more like feathers glued to wings than airfoils. Consultants, researchers, and practitioners often observe some successes, seek common attributes among them, and proclaim that those attributes can lead others to succeed. This simply does not work. You should be highly skeptical any time you see "the keys to success" or "formulas for winning."

Boeing's Nightmare: Outsourcing the Dreamliner

In the last few decades, many business consultants and companies have preached the virtues of outsourcing—the practice of contracting a previously in-house service to an outside company. Outsourcing may allow a firm to reduce its costs and capital intensity, desirable goals in a competitive world. And a number of the organizations that have outsourced, including Apple and Dell, have enjoyed terrific business and financial success. The correlation between outsourcing and fine results seemed clear.

Boeing, the world's largest airplane manufacturer, has long used outside suppliers. Traditionally, Boeing engineers designed a plane and sent the detailed blueprints to suppliers, a system they called "build-to-print." This process allowed Boeing to control key design and engineering functions while lowering overall costs. But for its newest plane, the 787 Dreamliner, Boeing opted to have the suppliers both design and build the airplane sections, leaving only the final assembly to its own mechanics. The company hoped to pare two years from its historical go-to-market time and envisioned assembling a 787 in just three days, one-tenth the normal time for a plane that size.

The program was a disaster. Despite being a best-seller with almost nine hundred orders, the plane saw its launch repeatedly delayed as the program slipped well over a year behind schedule. The problem was that the suppliers were unable to deliver fully functional sections of the plane for Boeing's final assembly. While Boeing designed the production system to integrate twelve hundred components, the first plane came in thirty thousand pieces, costing the company substantial time and money as it had to pull design work back in house.[7]

Boeing's problems with the 787 are symptomatic of the first decision mistake: embracing a strategy without fully understanding the conditions under which it succeeds or fails. Outsourcing is not universally good. For example, outsourcing does not make sense for products that require the complex integration of disparate subcomponents. The reason is that coordination costs are high, so just getting the product to work is a challenge. Think of IBM in the early days of the personal computer industry. The company made almost all its own components to ensure compatibility. In this stage, vertically integrated businesses do best.

Outsourcing does make sense for industries where subcomponents are modules. In these cases, the performance of the subcomponents is well defined, and the final assembly is straightforward. Today, you can build a personal computer yourself with standardized modules. Once an industry defines the modules, it makes more sense for suppliers to specialize in one component instead of trying to make them all. Assemblers like Dell can then focus on design, marketing, and distribution.

Before the 787, Boeing had controlled the design and engineering processes for its planes, ensuring the compatibility of the components and a smooth final assembly. But by ceding design and engineering to suppliers, Boeing's 787 program became a case study in when to avoid outsourcing. Boeing was drawn to outsourcing as an attribute, without fully recognizing the circumstances under which it would work.[8]

What Would Colonel Blotto Do? A Game of Strategy

I sometimes settle my children's squabbles—who gets to go first, who gets to sit where—by having them play the Colonel Blotto game. We use a simple version. Each player gets a hundred soldiers (resources) to distribute in three battlefields (dimensions). The players write their battlefield allocations secretly, and then we compare results. The player with the most soldiers per battlefield wins that battle, and the player with the most overall wins is the victor. Table 6-1 provides an example of a real game from my family. While there are a few really bad strategies in this version of the game

TABLE 6-1

Colonel Blotto game outcome

	Battlefield 1	Battlefield 2	Battlefield 3
Andrew	5	65	30
Alex	48	2	50
Winner	Alex	Andrew	Alex

(e.g., 100, 0, 0), the outcomes are for the most part random—a lot like rock, paper, scissors.[9] Colonel Blotto is applicable for military strategists, politicians, marketers, and sports-team managers.[10]

The Colonel Blotto game is useful because by varying the game's two main parameters, giving one player more resources or changing the number of battlefields, you can gain insight into the likely winners of competitive encounters. It shows when underdogs have the best chance to win, why there is sometimes no "best" team, and how changes in parameters influence those outcomes. Simply, the game offers insight into our second decision mistake, a failure to think properly about competitive circumstances. In the Colonel Blotto game, you can think of resources as attributes and dimensions as circumstances. The game provides perspective on how to evaluate outcomes across combinations of attributes and circumstances.

Let's look more closely at what happens when we alter the parameters. First, we can increase resource asymmetry by giving one player more points than the other, effectively making one side the favorite to win. It should come as no surprise that the stronger player wins more frequently. What's not as intuitive is how much advantage the additional points confer. In a three-battlefield game, a player with 25 percent more resources has a 60 percent expected payoff (the proportion of battles the player wins), and a player with twice the resources has a 78 percent expected payoff. So some randomness exists, even in contests with fairly asymmetric resources, but the resource-rich side has a decisive advantage. Further, with low dimensions, the game is largely transitive: if A can beat B and B can beat C, then A can beat C. Colonel Blotto helps us to understand games with few dimensions, such as tennis.

But to get the whole picture of the payoffs, we must introduce the second parameter, the number of dimensions or battlefields. The more dimensions the game has, the less certain the outcome (unless the players have identical resources). For example, a weak player's expected payoff is nearly three times higher in a game with fifteen dimensions than in a nine-dimension game.[11] For this reason, the outcome is harder to predict in a high-dimension game than in a low-dimension game, and as a result there are more upsets. Baseball is a good example of a high-dimension game. While the better team has an edge, the outcomes include a large dose of randomness. Year after year, winning 60 percent of the season's 162 games virtually guarantees a spot in the postseason playoffs.[12] Decision making and evaluating outcomes are markedly different in high-dimension games than in low-dimension games.

The Colonel Blotto game is also highly nontransitive in all but largely asymmetric, low-dimension situations.[13] For this reason, tournaments often fail to reveal a best team. Scott Page, a social scientist at the University of Michigan, illustrates the point with a simple example (see table 6-2). In this case, player A beats B, B beats C, C beats A, and all three players beat D. So if these players are in a tournament, the one who draws D in the first round will win it all. No best player exists; it is more accurate to describe the champion as "the player who got to play D first." Not so catchy, but accurate.[14]

Figure 6-1 summarizes some insights you can gain from studying the Colonel Blotto game. The stronger player wins most battles against the weaker player if the dimensionality is low. With equally matched players, the number of suboptimal strategies rises as

TABLE 6-2

Nontransitivity in the Colonel Blotto game

	Battlefield 1	Battlefield 2	Battlefield 3
Player A	40	20	40
Player B	35	40	25
Player C	20	35	45
Player D	33	33	34

Source: Scott E. Page, *The Difference* (Princeton, NJ: Princeton University Press, 2007). Reprinted by permission of the publisher.

FIGURE 6-1

High-dimension contests increase the uncertainty of outcomes

		Determinant outcomes	Quasi-determinant outcomes
Resource asymmetry	High	• Best player usually wins • Largely transitive	• Best player less dominant • Nontransitive
	Low	Random outcomes • Few suboptimal strategies • Nontransitive	Random outcomes • More suboptimal strategies • Nontransitive
		Low	High

Dimensionality

dimensions increase, because the players risk lumping resources in a few battlefields and thereby leaving a large number of battlefields without resources. But increasing the number of dimensions also dilutes the relative strength of the high-resource player. As military strategists have known for years, increasing the number of battle-fields often helps the underdog. Baseball has a lot more upsets than tennis for this reason. What is perhaps the most important lesson from the Colonel Blotto game is that you must be circumspect in evaluating decisions and outcomes. Because of nontransitivity and randomness, the attribute of resources does not always prevail over the circumstance of dimensionality. In a complex game, the best man doesn't necessarily win.

Correlation and Causality—*Not!*

Stock-market soothsayers are always looking for reliable ways to anticipate the market's direction. One favorite is the Super Bowl Indicator, invariably trotted out after the football season's championship game. The indicator is simple: the stock market goes up when a National Football Conference team wins and goes down when an American Football Conference team wins. The Super Bowl winner has correctly predicted the stock market's direction nearly 80 percent of the time from 1967 to 2008. Another is David Leinweber's analysis that shows a 75 percent correlation between butter production in Bangladesh and the level of the Standard & Poor's 500 Stock Index (1981–1993). Leinweber mined a wide range of international data series and was pleased to find that "a simple dairy product" explained so much.[15]

Leinweber used a silly example to make a serious point: the failure to distinguish between correlation and causality. This problem arises when researchers observe a correlation between two variables and assume that one *caused* the other. Once you are attuned to this mistake, you will see and hear it everywhere—especially in the media. Vegetarians have higher IQs. Nightlights lead to nearsightedness. Kids who watch too much television tend to be obese.

Numerous scholars from varied disciplines have studied causation, and most agree that three conditions must hold to make a claim that X causes Y.[16] The first is that X must occur before Y. The second is a functional relationship between X and Y, including the requirement that cause and effect take on two or more values. For example, the statement "smoking causes lung cancer" says that smoking increases the chances of lung cancer versus not smoking So a scientist must consider all the relationships between the variables: does the person smoke (yes or no) and does the person have cancer (yes or no). Here, too, you must consider whether the relationship is merely happenstance.

The final condition is that for X to cause Y, there cannot be a factor Z that causes both X and Y. For instance, watching too much television may correlate with obesity. But low socioeconomic status may explain *both* the television viewing and the weight problem.[17]

You must be very alert to the correlation-causality mistake. The fact that we like to make explicit cause-and-effect connections only adds to the challenge. When you hear of a causal connection, step carefully through the three conditions to see if the claim holds up. You will most likely be surprised at how rarely you can firmly establish causation.

I Did It My Way (and Died)

Scientists studying the Norse inhabitants of Greenland found the skull of a twenty-five-year-old man on the floor of a large house in the Eastern Settlement. Radiocarbon techniques dated the skull to around AD 1300, about four hundred years after the Norse first landed on Greenland's shores. As the custom was to bury the dead, the position of the man's body suggests that he was one of the last Norse inhabitants in the area. After four centuries of a challenging existence, the Greenland Norse society collapsed. One wonders how the society survived as long as it did.

Our chapter's final decision mistake—inflexibility in the face of evidence that change is necessary—helps to explain the Norse's demise. Jared Diamond's book *Collapse* tells the fascinating story of the group's tribulations and ultimate failure. Leaving aside many of the details, we can say that the Norse were inflexible in two important ways.[18]

First, the Norse sought to perpetuate their way of life from Norway and Iceland. As they doggedly applied what had worked in their homelands to their adopted land, they quickly depleted the few environmental resources that Greenland had to offer. They cut down too many trees (limiting fuel and building materials), stripped turf to build homes (leaving livestock with less to eat and causing erosion), and allowed overgrazing (damaging the region's flora). In retrospect, this ravaging makes no sense, but it was consistent with the Norse's self-image and experience.

Second, the Norse did not appear to learn from the native Inuit. Probably reflecting their attitudes as European Christians, the Norse scorned the Inuit and had a mostly antagonistic relationship with them. Even though the Inuit developed clever means to find food in Greenland's hardscrabble environment, the Norse did not imitate them. As Diamond notes, "The Norse starved in the presence of abundant unutilized food resources." They failed to fish, go whaling, and hunt ringed seals as the Inuit did. The values that had helped the society in a different environment now led to a nearly inexplicable inflexibility. And that inflexibility caused the last man to starve, as the others had done before him.

While the story of the Greenland Norse may seem like a historical curiosity, contemporary professional organizations continue to make the same mistakes. They perpetuate past practices as the world changes and refuse to embrace best practices from other organizations (often called the "not invented here syndrome"). Changing the decision-making process as circumstances dictate is a fundamental challenge and can be psychologically taxing.

Here are some thoughts on how you can make sure you are correctly considering circumstances in your decision making:

1. *Ask whether the theory behind your decision making accounts for circumstances.* People frequently attempt to extrapolate successful choices from prior experiences to new situations, with predictably poor results. Flawed research that draws common attributes from organizations that have done well and offers those attributes as a general prescription for winning is also popular. Neither mistake properly considers decisions in context.

   One positive example is an exercise that Thomas Thurston, a former Intel employee, completed in 2006. Steeped in the theory of disruptive innovation, which is based on circumstances, Thurston reviewed almost fifty business plans that Intel's new business initiatives group had funded. Applying the theory that specifies when innovations succeed, he was able to predict, without knowledge of the outcomes, a statistically significant 85 percent of successes and failures.[19] Further, he was able to identify where some of the failed businesses had gone wrong. Thurston then teamed up with Clayton Christensen to teach the theory to business school students. Their first pass at sorting the winners and losers was close to random, but by the end of the semester the students sorted with over 80 percent accuracy. The progress shows the theory's value and that the students can learn the lessons and improve performance.

2. *Watch for the correlation-and-causality trap.* People have an
    innate desire to link cause and effect and are not beyond mak-
    ing up a cause for the effects they see. This creates the risk of
    observing a correlation—often the result of chance—and
    assuming causation. When you hear of a correlation, be sure
    to consider the three conditions: time precedence, relation-
    ship, and that no additional factor is causing the other two to
    correlate.

3. *Balance simple rules with changing conditions.* Evolution
    provides a powerful argument for circumstance-based
    thinking. In evolution, the ability of an individual to survive
    and reproduce does not simply reflect specific attributes like
    size, color, or strength. Rather, the inherited characteristics
    that lead to survival and reproduction are inherently cir-
    cumstantial. One approach to decision making—especially
    for rapidly changing environments—balances a handful of
    simple but definite rules with the prevailing conditions. For
    example, priority rules help managers rank the opportuni-
    ties they identify, or exit rules tell them when to leave a
    business. The rules make sure that managers uphold certain
    core ideals while recognizing changing conditions, allowing
    for the requisite flexibility to decide properly.[20]

4. *Remember there is no "best" practice in domains with multi-
    ple dimensions.* While many people, especially Westerners,
    are keen to determine which organization is best, crowning
    a winner in a high-dimensionality realm makes no sense.
    One of the Colonel Blotto game's main lessons is that under
    most circumstances, winning strategies are nontransitive:
    all players have strengths and weaknesses, leaving no indi-
    vidual player dominant against all comers. Further, the
    game shows that an underdog hitting on the right strategy
    can slay the favorite.

    An illustration comes from the 2002 Super Bowl, which
    pitted the New England Patriots against the St. Louis Rams.

The Rams had outplayed the Patriots when the teams met during the regular season and were heavy favorites to win the championship. But the Patriots radically shifted their strategy for the Super Bowl. Instead of dwelling on the quarterback, Kurt Warner, as they had in their prior meeting, the Patriots focused on stopping the running back, Marshall Faulk. They recognized that the Rams relied on timing and rhythm in their offense and that it was Faulk, not Warner, who was key.

The strategy worked brilliantly, leading to an improbable Patriots victory and prompting Ron Jaworski, one of football's most respected commentators, to pronounce it "the best coaching job I've ever seen." Of course, by allocating a great deal of resources to one battle, the Patriots left themselves open to losing other battles. The strategy called for the Patriots to use five or more defensive backs almost three-quarters of the time. Because backs are smaller than other defensive players, the Patriots became susceptible to being overpowered. However, the Rams head coach opted not to run the ball, determined to "win it my way," frustrating his imploring players.[21] Oh, and the stock market went down in 2002—the Patriots are an American Football Conference team—adding another favorable datapoint to the Super Bowl Indicator.

Most of us look forward to leveraging our favorable experiences by applying the same approach to the next situation. We also have a thirst for success formulas—key steps to enrich ourselves. Sometimes our experience and nostrums work, but more often they fail us. The reason usually boils down to the simple reality that the theories guiding our decisions are based on attributes, not circumstances. Attribute-based theories come very naturally to us and often appear compelling, as we saw with the birth-order discussion. However, once you realize the answer to most questions is, "It depends," you are ready to embark on the quest to figure out what it depends *on*.

CHAPTER SEVEN

Grand Ah-Whooms

How Ten Brits Made the Millennium Bridge Wobble

O N A SUNNY DAY IN 2000, the Queen of England dedicated the Millennium Bridge to the sounds of fanfare. London's first new bridge over the river Thames since 1894, it connects the City and St. Paul's Cathedral on the north with the Tate and the Globe Theatre on the south. Selected from over two hundred entries in a global contest, the winning design was fresh and contemporary and pushed the boundaries of art, architecture, and engineering. The bridge's architect, Norman Foster, envisioned pedestrians enjoying the thrill of "walking on water in a blade of light."[1]

Foster collaborated on the project with Arup, an engineering firm, and Anthony Caro, a sculptor. They sought to build an exceptionally flat and sleek bridge, one that was 325 meters long but with only minimal cable sag. After spending close to £20 million, the team appeared to have blended a beautiful aesthetic design with rigorous engineering requirements. The bridge met all international bridge standards, was built to specifications, and Arup did all the construction calculations correctly.

One hundred thousand people showed up for the bridge's public opening on June 10, vastly more than officials expected. The first sign of trouble appeared at a preopening walk that morning, when a smattering of people filled the bridge. One of Arup's engineers noticed some movement, but the bridge settled down as the numbers thinned. The bridge officially opened to the public at lunchtime, and crowds swarmed on from both ends. The bridge soon started to wobble as much as seven centimeters from side to side, causing the unsuspecting pedestrians to widen their stances and synchronize their gaits. The video of the scene looks like a mob of penguins inching along.

Naturally, the bridge's builders were well aware of crowd forces; you may have heard about marching armies breaking step as they cross a bridge. Whereas vertical movement is the typical engineering concern, the Millennium Bridge's problem was lateral motion. One bridge crosser described the unusual sensation of instability as "rather like being on a boat" (see figure 7-1). Though structurally safe, the bridge was closed for retrofitting just two days after

FIGURE 7-1

The Millennium Bridge swayed side-to-side on opening day

Source: Getty Images.

its heralded opening, to the embarrassment of the whole project team and the city of London.[2]

While fixing the bridge, workers erected temporary gates and pinned up signs that read: "Bridge Closed." Next to the sign on the north side, a passerby dashed a single word: "Why?"[3]

When the Positive Feedback Takes Over

Feedback can be negative or positive, and within many systems you see a healthy balance of the two. Negative feedback is a stabilizing factor, while positive feedback promotes change. But too much of either type of feedback can leave a system out of balance.

The classic illustration of negative feedback in markets is arbitrage. For instance, if the price of gold in London drifts a little above the price in New York, arbitrageurs will buy New York gold and sell London gold until they close the aberrant price gap. A more mundane example is your thermostat, which detects deviations from the temperature you set and sends instructions to return the temperature back to your desired level. Negative feedback resists change by pushing in the opposite direction.

Positive feedback reinforces an initial change in the same direction. Imagine a school of fish or a flock of birds eluding a predator. They move in unison to avoid the threat. We also see positive feedback at work in fads and fashions, where people imitate one another. Positive feedback can explain bouts with Pet Rocks, the Macarena, and Pokémon cards.

The focus of this chapter is phase transitions, where small incremental changes in causes lead to large-scale effects. Philip Ball, a physicist and writer, calls it the *grand ah-whoom*.[4] Put a tray of water into your freezer and the temperature drops to the threshold of freezing. The water remains a liquid until—*ah-whoom*—it becomes ice. Just a small incremental change in temperature leads to a change from liquid to solid.

The grand ah-whoom occurs in many complex systems where collective behavior emerges from the interaction of its constituent parts. You can find lots of these systems in the physical world, including water molecules and iron atoms. But the ideas also apply to the social world, even though the laws aren't defined as clearly as they are in physics. Examples include everything from the behavior of stock exchanges to the popularity of hit songs.

To be clear, in all these systems cause and effect are proportionate most of the time. But they also have critical points, or thresholds, where phase transitions occur. You can think of these points as occurring when one form of feedback overwhelms the other. When you don't see it coming, the grand ah-whoom will surprise you.[5]

Let's use the idea of a phase transition to answer the question that was scrawled on the sign at the Millennium Bridge. When you walk, your mass exerts a small amount of sideways force. These individual forces normally cancel out when a group crosses a stiff bridge, an example of negative feedback. However, the Millennium Bridge initially had insufficient lateral dampeners, allowing a little swaying when enough people were on the bridge. That swaying forced people to change their gait by widening their steps. The wider steps lead to greater sideways force and more swaying. The positive feedback caused the wobbling and synchronized crowd behavior to emerge simultaneously.[6]

The vital insight is the existence of a critical point. In December 2000, Arup engineers enlisted volunteers to walk on the bridge in order to determine the level at which the unsafe swaying would occur. Their test showed that 156 people could walk on the bridge with little impact (see figure 7-2). But adding just 10 more pedestrians caused the amplitude to change dramatically, as the positive feedback kicked in (see figure 7-2 right axis). For the first 156 people who crossed the bridge, there was little sway and no sense of any potential hazard, even though the bridge was on the cusp of a phase transition.

This shows why critical points are so important for proper counterfactual thinking: considering what might have been.[7] For every phase transition you do see, how many close calls were there? You can imagine testing the bridge with 50, 100, or even 150 people. The

FIGURE 7-2

The outbreak of wobbling on the Millennium Bridge was sudden

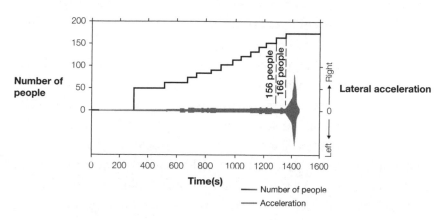

Source: http://www.arup.com/MillenniumBridge/.

harmful wobble lies in the wait, outside of your awareness. The large-scale outcome is due to the internal workings of the system—people walking—not from some external shock. But the risk is real. I call this invisible vulnerability.

Critical Points, Extremes, and Surprise

With lots of phenomena, including human heights and athletic results, the outcomes don't stray too far from average. Take heights as an example. The tallest human on record grew to a height of 272 centimeters (8'11"), while the shortest was 57 centimeters (1'10"), a roughly five-to-one differential. Approximately 95 percent of people vary no more than 15 centimeters (about 6 inches) from the average height. Heights have a narrow and predictable range of outcomes.

But there are systems with heavily skewed distributions, where the idea of average holds little or no meaning. These distributions are better described by a power law, which implies that a few of the outcomes are really large (or have a large impact) and most observations are small. Look at city sizes. New York City, with about 8 million inhabitants, is the largest city in the United States. The smallest town has about 50 people. So the ratio of the largest to the smallest is more than 150,000 to 1. Other social phenomena, like book or movie sales, show such extreme differences as well. City sizes have a much wider range of outcomes than human heights do.[8]

Nassim Taleb, an author and former derivatives trader, calls the extreme outcomes within power law distributions *black swans*. He defines a black swan as an outlier event that has a consequential impact and that humans seek to explain after the fact.[9] In large part owing to Taleb's efforts, more people are aware of black swans and distributions that deviate from the bell curve. What most people still don't appreciate is the mechanism that propagates black swans.

Here's where critical points and phase transitions come in. Positive feedback leads to outcomes that are outliers. And critical points help explain our perpetual surprise at black swan events because we have a hard time understanding how such small incremental perturbations can lead to such large outcomes. We simply don't see them coming because they are beyond what our minds expect.

What is behind these critical points in social systems? One answer comes from studying the wisdom of crowds.[10] Crowds tend to make accurate predictions when three conditions prevail— diversity, aggregation, and incentives. Diversity is about people having different ideas and different views of things. Aggregation means you can bring the group's information together. Incentives are rewards for being right and penalties for being wrong that are often, but not necessarily, monetary.

For a host of psychological and sociological reasons, diversity is the most likely condition to fail when humans are involved. But what's essential is that the crowd doesn't go from smart to dumb gradually. As you slowly remove diversity, nothing happens initially. Additional reductions may also have no effect. But at a certain critical point, a small incremental reduction causes the system to change qualitatively.

Blake LeBaron, an economist at Brandeis University, has demonstrated this point for the stock market using an agent-based model. Instead of using real investors, LeBaron's model created a thousand investors within the computer and gave them money, guidelines on allocating their portfolios, and diverse trading rules. Then he let them loose.

His model was able to replicate many of the empirical features we see in the real world, including cycles of booms and crashes. But perhaps his most important finding is that a stock price can continue to rise even while the diversity of decision rules falls. Invisible vulnerability grows. But then, *ah-whoom*, the stock price tumbles as diversity rises again. Writes LeBaron, "During the run-up to a crash, population diversity falls. Agents begin using very similar trading strategies as their common good performance is reinforced. This makes the population very brittle, in that a small reduction in the demand for shares could have a strong destabilizing impact on the market."[11]

The Problem of Induction, Reductive Bias, and Bad Predictions

The presence of phase transitions invites a few common decision-making mistakes. The first is the problem of induction, or how you should logically go from specific observations to general conclusions. Although philosophers, from Sextus Empiricus to David Hume, have for centuries warned against extrapolating from what we see, refraining from doing so is very difficult. To state the obvious, induction fails —sometimes spectacularly so— in systems with phase transitions.

To illustrate the problem, Taleb retells Bertrand Russell's story of a turkey that is fed a thousand days in a row. (Russell actually spoke of a chicken. Taleb changed it to a turkey for the American audience.)[12] The feedings reinforce the turkey's sense of security and well-being, until the day before Thanksgiving an unexpected event occurs. All the turkey's experience and feedback is positive until fortune takes a turn for the worse.

The equivalent of the turkey's plight—sharp losses following a period of prosperity—has occurred repeatedly in business. For example, Merrill Lynch (which was acquired by Bank of America) suffered losses over a two-year period from 2007 to 2008 that were in excess of one-third of the profits it had earned cumulatively in its thirty-six years as a public company.[13] Dealing with a system governed by a power law is like the farmer feeding us while he holds the axe behind his back. If you stick around long enough, the axe will fall. The question is not if, but when.

The term *black swan* reflects the criticism of induction by the philosopher Karl Popper. Popper argued that seeing lots of white swans doesn't prove the theory that all swans are white, but seeing one black swan does disprove it. So Popper's point is that to understand a phenomenon, we're better off focusing on falsification than on verification. But we're not naturally inclined to falsify something.

Karl Duncker, a psychologist, observed that when people use or think about something in a particular way they have great difficulty thinking about it in new ways. In a classic experiment, Duncker gave subjects a candle, a box of tacks, and a pack of matches. He then asked them to attach the candle to a wall so that it wouldn't drip on the table below. The trick was to use the tack box as a platform, something few participants thought to do. Duncker argued that people fixate on an object's normal function and could not conceptualize it differently. People have a strong tendency to stick to an established perspective and are slow to consider alternatives.

Repeated, good outcomes provide us with confirming evidence that our strategy is good and everything is fine. This illusion lulls us into an unwarranted sense of confidence and sets us up for a (usually negative) surprise. The fact that phase transitions come with sudden change only adds to the confusion.

Another mistake that we make when dealing with complex systems is what psychologists call reductive bias, "a tendency for people to treat and interpret complex circumstances and topics as simpler than they really are, leading to misconception."[14] When asked to decide about a system that's complex and nonlinear, a person will often revert to thinking about a system that is simple and linear. Our minds naturally offer an answer to a related but easier question, often with costly consequences.

Finance offers a great example of this bias. While empirical research from as early as the 1920s showed that changes in the price of assets do not follow a normal, bell-shaped distribution, economic theory still rests on that assumption. If you have ever heard a financial expert refer to the stock market using terms like alpha, beta, or standard deviation, you have witnessed reductive bias in action. Most economists characterize markets using simpler, but wrong, price-change distributions. A number of high-profile financial blow-ups, including Long-Term Capital Management, show the danger of this bias.[15]

Benoit Mandelbrot, a French mathematician and the father of fractal geometry, was one of the earliest and most vocal critics of using normal distributions to explain how asset prices move.[16] His chapter in *The Random Character of Stock Market Prices*, published in 1964, created a stir because it demonstrated that asset price changes were much more extreme than previous models had assumed. Paul Cootner, an economist at MIT and the editor of the volume, was unconvinced of Mandelbrot's case. "If [Mandelbrot] is right," he wrote, "almost all of our statistical tools are obsolete. Almost without exception, past econometric work is meaningless."[17]

But Cootner could rest easy, because Mandelbrot's ideas never penetrated mainstream economics. Philip Mirowski, a historian and philosopher of economic thought at Notre Dame, notes, "The simple historical fact is that [Mandelbrot's economic ideas] have been by and large ignored, with some few exceptions ... which seem to have been subsequently abandoned by their authors."[18]

A few years ago, I went to a dinner in New York City that included Mandelbrot. I showed up late and saw just two seats free. Mandelbrot arrived shortly after me and explained that his tardiness was due to an incompetent driver, whom he fired. Mandelbrot then leaned over and asked, "Would you mind giving me a ride home?"

I fretted for the rest the dinner, wondering what I could possibly say to this remarkable man forty years my senior during an hour-long drive to the suburbs. As he slipped into the passenger seat, I decided to ask him about the history of reductive bias in finance. He was very gracious, albeit frustrated that the establishment had yet to accept his point of view. While the market's wild randomness was there for all to see, he said, economists stuck with mild randomness, in large part because it simplified the world and made the math more tractable. Mandelbrot emphasized that while he didn't know what extreme event was going to happen in the future, he was sure that the simple models of the economists would not anticipate it.

Well, it didn't take long. The financial crisis of 2007–2009 had a lot of moving parts but near the center was a little-known formula developed by David Li, a statistician and mathematician. The equation deals with the tricky challenge of measuring the correlation of default between assets. (The formula is known as a Gaussian copula function.)

Correlation is crucial in diversifying a portfolio and, hence, in managing risk. For example, consider two potential investments: Umbrella Corp. and Picnic Basket Inc. If the weather is inclement, Umbrella Corp.'s stock goes up and Picnic Basket Inc.'s stock goes down. Of course, nice weather leads to the opposite market reaction. Because the performance of the stocks is not correlated, you'll be diversified if you own both no matter the weather. But if the stocks become correlated—they both go up or down at the same time for whatever reason—you'll be exposed to more risk than you thought.

The promise of Li's equation was that it could, with a single number, measure the likelihood that two or more assets within a portfolio would default at the same time. This opened the floodgates for new products, as financial engineers had a method for quantifying the safety or riskiness of a security that bundled lots of assets. For example, an investment bank could bundle corporate bonds into a pool, known as a collateralized debt obligation, and summarize the default correlation with Li's equation rather than worry about the details of how each corporate bond within the pool would behave.

While market participants described the formula as "beautiful, simple, and tractable," it had a fatal flaw because correlations change. Consistent with reductive bias, the equation was based on an uncomplicated, stable world but was applied in a complex, dynamic world. As is often the case, default correlations rise when the economy turns south.

The failure of Long-Term Capital Management illustrates how changing correlations can wreak havoc. LTCM observed that the correlation between its diverse investments was less than 10 percent over the prior five years. To stress test its portfolio, LTCM assumed that correlations could rise to 30 percent, well in excess of anything the historical data showed. But when the financial crisis hit in 1998, the correlations soared to 70 percent. Diversification went out the window, and the fund suffered mortal losses. "Anything that relies on correlation is charlatanism," scoffed Taleb. Or, as I've heard traders say, "The only thing that goes up in a bear market is correlation."[19]

The final mistake in dealing with phase transitions is the belief in prediction. Ours is the only world we know. But it is tantalizing to ask whether outcomes would be different if we went back in time and replayed the tape.[20] Would evolution still have produced trees and dogs and people? And if models of how people adopt ideas and innovations suggest a large role for serendipity, how can we know about what could have been? Or what will be?

Generally, there is no way to test the inevitability of the outcomes we see. However, a trio of researchers at Columbia University, led by Duncan Watts, a sociologist, conducted a study that essentially fashioned multiple worlds to see how people behave in various social settings. We may not be able to replay the history of our world, but the scientists effectively created alternative universes.[21] The findings of Watts and his colleagues give pause to anyone in the prediction business.

They created a Web site called Music Lab and invited subjects to participate in a study of musical tastes. The site asked subjects to listen to and rate forty-eight songs by unknown bands, with an option to download the songs they liked. Over fourteen thousand people participated, mostly young people residing in the United States.

Upon entering the site, the researchers assigned 20 percent of the subjects to an independent world and 10 percent each to eight worlds where people were allowed to see what other people were doing (see figure 7-3). In the independent world, subjects listened to and rated the songs and were free to download them, but had no information about what others were doing. In the other worlds the subjects also listened to and rated songs, but social influence came into play because they could see how many times other people had downloaded each song. The researchers ran a couple variations of the experiment, but in all scenarios the songs started with zero downloads.

The study's setup allowed for a very explicit test of social influence. The subjects in the independent group, unswayed by the

FIGURE 7-3

How Music Lab created alternative worlds

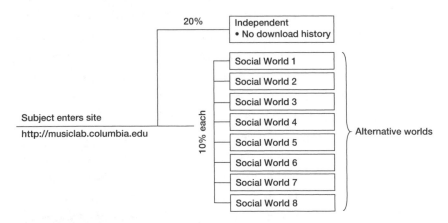

Source: Based on Duncan J. Watts, "Is Justin Timberlake a Product of Cumulative Advantage?" *New York Times Magazine,* April 15, 2007.

opinion of others, provided a reasonable indicator of the quality of the songs. If social influence is inconsequential, you would expect the song rankings—and downloads—to be similar in all nine worlds. On the other hand, if social influence is important, small differences in the initial download pattern in the social worlds would lead to very different rankings. Cumulative advantage would trump intrinsic quality.

The study showed that song quality did play a role in the ranking. A top-five song in the independent world had about a 50 percent chance of finishing in the top five in a social influence world. And the worst songs rarely topped the charts. But how would you guess an average song performed in the social worlds? Do you think the opinions of others would shape your taste?

The scientists found that social influence played a huge part in success and failure. One song, "Lockdown" by the band 52metro, ranked twenty-sixth in the independent world, effectively average. Yet it was the number one song in one of the social influence worlds, and number forty in another. Social influence catapulted an average song to hit status in one world—*ah-whoom*—and delegated it to the cellar in another. Call it Lockdown's lesson.

In the eight social worlds, the songs the subjects downloaded early in the experiment had a huge influence on the songs subjects downloaded later. Since the patterns of download were different in each social world, so were the outcomes.

The Polya urn process offers insight into these outcomes.[22] Imagine a large urn with two balls inside, one red and one blue. You reach in and randomly select a ball. Say you pick the blue one. You then introduce one matching blue ball and return both balls to the urn (the urn now contains one red ball and two blue balls). You repeat the process, randomly selecting a ball, matching, and replacing until the urn is full. You then calculate the ratio of red to blue balls. Figure 7-4 shows six trial runs I simulated, each with one hundred rounds of remove and replace.

The urn process has features that fit nicely with Music Lab's results. First, for any individual trial run, you have no way of know-

ing the outcome ahead of time. The ratio can be skewed toward red
or blue, and multiple trials yield different ratios. As a result, it is
really hard to predict winners. While it is true that better-quality
products have a higher probability of success in the real world,
there is no assured link between commercial success and quality.
Further, social influence tends to exacerbate product successes and
failures, leading to extremes. In the Music Lab experiment, the
inequality of outcomes was substantially greater in the social
worlds than in the independent world.

Second, flexibility decreases over time. Once you've selected one
blue ball, the chances that you'll select another increases sharply.
If you happen to choose a blue ball just one or two more times, it
quickly becomes nearly impossible for red to dominate—all for
purely statistical reasons. While the eventual outcomes were

FIGURE 7-4

Outcomes vary widely in the Polya urn process

Six Trial Runs, 100 Rounds Each.

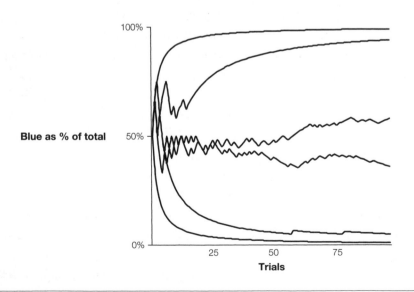

unclear early on in the Music Lab experiment, the results were stable once established there as well. For the social worlds, the outcomes stabilized after about one-third of the subjects participated. Like the urn, the luck of the initial draw was defining.

Finally, there is a memory effect. The color of the first ball that is selected strongly influences the outcome. Likewise, the first person to download a song influences the pattern of later downloads. Our world represents one of many possible worlds, and small changes in initial conditions lead to a big difference in outcomes. A scan of the ranking differences in the various social influence worlds attests to this.

To be clear, the Polya urn process is too simple to fully represent the Music Lab experiment and most social processes.[23] For example, the urn process is limited to two choices, while the experiment and real world are vastly more complicated. But the urn process does show how positive feedback leads to lopsided, unpredictable outcomes. Social influence can be the engine for positive feedback.

Recognizing the role of social influence in other domains is not difficult. Researchers have demonstrated the importance of cumulative advantage in the success of technologies, behaviors, and ideas. Classic examples include the battles for standard formats including Qwerty versus Dvorak typewriter keyboards, VHS versus Betamax video tapes, and Blu-ray Disc versus HD-DVD disks.[24] Each realm faces the same lack of predictability and loose correlation between success and quality. Each realm has critical points and phase transitions. In cases where cause and effect are not clear, learning from history is a challenge.

Here are some tips on how to cope with systems that have phase transitions:

1. *Study the distribution of outcomes for the system you are dealing with.* Thanks to Taleb's prodding, many people now associate extreme events with black swans. But Taleb makes a careful, if overlooked, distinction: if we

understand what the broader distribution looks like, the outcomes—however extreme—are correctly labeled as gray swans, not black swans. He calls them "modelable extreme events." In fact, scientists have done a lot of work classifying the distributions of various systems, including the stock market, terrorist acts, and power-grid failures.[25] So if you have the background and tools to understand these systems, you can get a general view of how the system behaves, even if you have no reliable means of predicting any specific event. The key is to properly prepare for whatever the system metes out, extreme or not. For the most part, people are scorched not by black swans, the unknown unknowns, but rather by their failure to prepare for gray swans.

2. *Look for ah-whoom moments.* As the discussion about the Millennium Bridge and the wisdom of crowds revealed, big changes in collective systems often occur when the system actors coordinate their behavior. Think of the dot-com boom of the late 1990s or the economic mess of 2007–2009. While a reduction in diversity does not guarantee a system change (although it does invoke invisible vulnerability), it substantially raises the probability. Coordinated behavior is at the core of many asymmetric outcomes, including favorable (best-selling books, venture capital) and unfavorable (national security, lending) outcomes. Be mindful of the level of diversity and recognize that state changes often come suddenly.

3. *Beware of forecasters.* Humans have a large appetite for forecasts and predictions across a broad spectrum of domains. People must recognize that the accuracy of forecasts in systems with phase transitions is dismal, even by so-called experts. Watts says, "We think there is something we can call quality . . . and the results we see in the world reflect this quality." But, he added, "I am comfortable with

the idea that the outcomes we get are often largely arbitrary."[26] The best course is to recognize the nature of the distribution and to prepare for all contingencies.

4. *Mitigate the downside, capture the upside.* One common and conspicuous error in dealing with complex systems is betting too much on a particular outcome. In the 1950s, John Kelly, a physicist at Bell Labs, developed a formula for optimal betting strategy based on information theory. The Kelly formula tells you how much to bet, given your edge. One of the Kelly formula's central lessons is that betting too much in a system with extreme outcomes leads to ruin. Betting too much explains the demise of many large financial institutions, including American International Group (AIG), which implicitly failed to consider extreme outcomes. For example, AIG, a large and profitable insurance company, moved aggressively into the derivatives business in order to improve profits. A sizable percentage of the business included selling insurance against defaults on assets tied to corporate debt and mortgage securities. When the market plunged in 2008, AIG was unable to meet its financial commitments and had to be bailed out by the US government. And none of AIG's models saw it coming.[27]

Highly improbable and extreme events come in both positive and negative flavors. In dealing with systems of collectives, the ideal is to get cost-effective exposure to positive events and to insure against negative events. While we are getting more sophisticated, the financial instruments that we see in the market that are tied to extreme events are often mispriced.[28] In the end, the admonishment of investment legend Peter Bernstein should carry the day: "Consequences are more important than probabilities." This does not mean you should focus on outcomes instead of process; it means you should consider all possible outcomes in your process.[29]

Increasingly, people must deal with systems that are marked by abrupt, unforeseeable change and rare but extreme outcomes. We are all particularly mistake-prone with these systems because we intuitively want to treat the system as being simpler than it is and to extrapolate the past into the future. Flag these systems when you see them, and slow down your decision-making procedures. Especially when navigating among adverse black swans, the key is to live to see another day.

CHAPTER EIGHT

Sorting Luck from Skill

Why Investors Excel at Buying High and Selling Low

THE BOSS BLEW HIS STACK. After the storied New York Yankees won only four of their first twelve games in 2005, George Steinbrenner, the baseball team's owner, could not contain his frustration. "I am bitterly disappointed by the lack of performance of our team," he seethed. "It is unbelievable to me that the highest-paid team in baseball would start the season in such a deep funk. They have the talent to win and they are not winning." Even with 93 percent of the season to go, Joe Torre, the team's manager, could only agree, "He's not saying anything we certainly don't know ourselves. When he does spend the money, he expects more than he's obviously gotten so far."[1]

The Yankees did come through, tying for first place in their division during the regular season, but not because of the Boss's tongue-lashing. But how much was because of skill, and how much was due to luck? Hard to say. We have difficulty sorting skill and luck in lots of fields, including business and investing. As a result, we make a host of predictable and natural mistakes, such as failing to appreciate the team's or the individual's inevitable reversion to the mean. This chapter will offer you a fresh perspective for interpreting your own team's winning streaks and slumps—or, for that matter, the performance of employees, business units, stockbrokers, and other professionals as individuals and groups.

Sweet Peas in the 1800s: A Brief History

Francis Galton, cousin of Charles Darwin, was a Victorian polymath who liked to count things. Curious about a broad range of topics including evolution, psychology, and meteorology, he brought an empiricist's discipline to testing his ideas. During his life, he gathered and analyzed a huge amount of data.

Through a process of inquiry and investigation, Galton discovered the phenomenon of reversion to the mean, a towering achievement in statistics.

The idea is that for many types of systems, an outcome that is not average will be followed by an outcome that has an expected value closer to the average. While most people recognize the idea of reversion to the mean, they often ignore or misunderstand the concept, leading to a slew of mistakes in their analysis.[2]

Galton's interest in this topic started with the idea that genius was inherited. He noticed that geniuses—musicians, artists, scientists—were way above the average, and that while their children were above the average, they were closer to it. Genius, however, was hard to measure. So Galton turned to something he could measure: sweet peas. He separated sweet pea seeds by size and showed that while the offspring tended to resemble the parent seed, their average size was closer to the mean of the full population.[3]

While normal, or bell-shaped, distributions were well known at that time, thinkers of the day generally assumed that the distributions were the result of a large number of small errors around an average. For instance, numerous scientists might make an estimate of a planet's position. Each estimate captures the position with some error, reflecting imperfect instruments or calculation. If those errors are as likely to be in one direction as another, they will cancel out, and the average of the estimates will be the planet's true position.

But the theory of errors could not explain Galton's findings. He recognized there had to be a different mechanism at work. Heredity clearly played an important role in determining the size of the peas;

it wasn't simply that errors were distributed around some sort of universal average.

So Galton rolled up his sleeves and embarked on a detailed study of stature. Galton gathered the heights of four hundred parents and more than nine hundred of their grown children. He combined the heights of the mothers and fathers into what he called "mid-parent stature" and found that they followed a normal distribution. He then calculated the height of their children and found that they reverted to the mean. Tall parents tend to have tall children. But the height of the children is closer to the average of all children. Short parents generally have short children. But those children are taller than their parents (see figure 8-1). This data allowed Galton to demonstrate and define reversion to the mean.[4]

FIGURE 8-1

Reversion to the mean in human heights

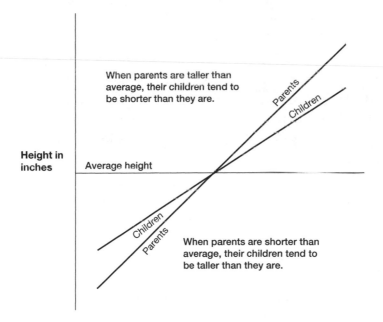

Source: Based on Francis Galton, "Regression towards Mediocrity in Hereditary Stature," *Journal of the Anthropological Institute* 15 (1886): 246–263.

Galton's significant insight was that, even as reversion to the mean occurs from one generation to the next, the *overall* distribution of heights remains stable over time. This combination sets a trap for people because reversion to the mean suggests things become more average over time, while a stable distribution implies things don't change much. Fully grasping how change and stability go together is the key to understanding reversion to the mean.[5]

Skill, Luck, and Outcomes

In many human endeavors, the outcomes are a combination of skill and luck. In baseball, for example, a pitcher can hurl a great game and yet his team may lose due to chance events. Naturally, the amount of influence that skill and luck will have depends on the activity. There is no skill involved in playing a slot machine. But winning at chess requires a great deal of skill and only a small amount of luck. Yet even when a player's skill doesn't change, his luck will come and go.

For example, consider how a golfer may score on two rounds on different days. If the golfer scores well below his handicap for the first round, how would you expect him to do for the second one? The answer is not as well. The exceptional score on the first round resulted from his being skillful but also very lucky. Even if he is just as skillful while playing the second round, you would not expect the same good luck.[6]

Any system that combines skill and luck will revert to the mean over time. Daniel Kahneman neatly captured this idea when he was asked to offer a formula for the twenty-first century. He actually provided two. Here's what he submitted:[7]

Success = Some talent + luck
Great success = Some talent + a lot of luck

Naturally, poor outcomes can reflect the combination of some skill and a lot of bad luck. That was the case with the first dozen games for the Yankees in 2005. However, over time, skill shines through as luck evens out, which helps explain why the Yankees finished in first place. Steinbrenner's view of his team was too narrow. He saw that the Yankees had lost eight of twelve games. But he didn't take into account that the Yankees were among the most skillful ballplayers in the nation (even though he was paying their sizable salaries). They started to win when their luck improved.

When you ignore the concept of reversion to the mean, you make three types of mistakes. The first mistake is thinking you're special. I once met with a company's senior management team and discussed my interpretation of reversion to the mean in corporate performance. The executives all nodded knowingly. Then the CEO chimed in, "Yes, we understand the idea of mean reversion well. But it doesn't apply to *us* because we've figured out a better way to run our business." If it were only so.

One example of ignoring reversion to the mean comes from the world of investing. Which investment manager would you rather hire: the one who recently beat the market or the one who lagged behind the index? Of course, there is no easy answer. Luck clearly plays a large but elusive role in how much money you'll make from any investment, especially in the short term. But even though industry pros intellectually understand the importance of luck, they consistently fail to incorporate that knowledge into their decisions.

Amit Goyal, a finance professor at Emory University, and Sunil Wahal, a finance professor at Arizona State University, analyzed how thirty-four hundred retirement plans, endowments, and foundations (plan sponsors) hired and fired firms that manage investment funds over a ten-year period. The researchers found that plan sponsors tended to hire managers who had performed well in the recent past. And the number one reason to fire a manager was poor performance. Consistent with reversion to the mean, the researchers noted that in subsequent years, many of the managers who were fired went on to outperform the managers who were hired (see figure 8-2).[8]

Individual investors behave similarly. Individuals earn returns that are generally 50 percent to 75 percent of the S&P 500 Index

FIGURE 8-2

Hire them when they are hot and hold them when they are not

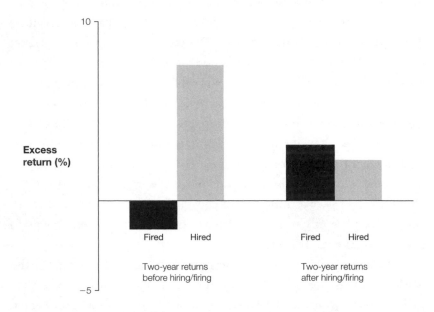

Source: Amit Goyal and Sunil Wahal, "The Selection and Termination of Investment Management Firms by Plan Sponsors," *Journal of Finance* 63, no. 4 (2008): 1805–1847.

precisely because they pour money into hot markets and yank it out after a drop. They buy high and sell low. Those people who ignore reversion to the mean forgo substantial investment returns on their hard-earned money.[9]

In my research, I found that analysts on Wall Street ignore the effects of reversion to the mean when they build their models of a company's future financial results. Analysts regularly neglect the evidence for reversion to the mean in considering essential drivers like company sales growth rates and levels of economic profitability.[10]

Secrist's Blunder

"Mediocrity tends to prevail in the conduct of competitive business," wrote Horace Secrist, an economist at Northwestern University, in his 1933 book, *The Triumph of Mediocrity in Business*. With that stroke of the pen, Secrist became a lasting example of the second mistake associated with reversion to the mean—a misinterpretation of what the data says.[11] Secrist's book is truly impressive. Its four hundred-plus pages show mean-reversion in series after series in an apparent affirmation of the tendency toward mediocrity. My research gives an example of Secrist's idea. Figure 8-3 shows how the spread between return on invested capital (ROIC) and cost of capital reverts to the mean for a sample of more than a thousand companies, broken into quintiles, over a decade (the figure tracks the median ROIC for each quintile). While contemporary, this picture would have fit comfortably inside Secrist's text.[12]

Secrist's book was warmly received for the most part, with the notable exception of a scathing review by Harold Hotelling, an economist and statistician at Columbia University. The problem, Hotelling pointed out, is "these diagrams really prove nothing more than the ratios in question have a tendency to wander about."[13] The best visual for understanding Hotelling's criticism is figure 8-4. At the top is the distribution of ROICs for the sample in 1997. In the middle is the reversion to the mean from figure 8-3, and on the bottom is

FIGURE 8-3

Corporate returns on invested capital mean revert (1997–2007)

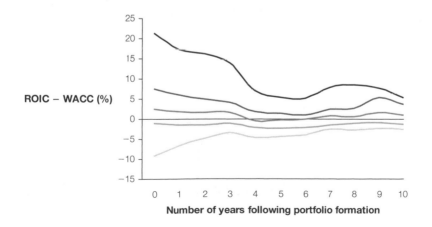

FIGURE 8-4

Reversion to the mean does not imply the triumph of mediocrity

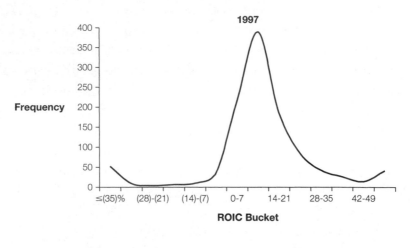

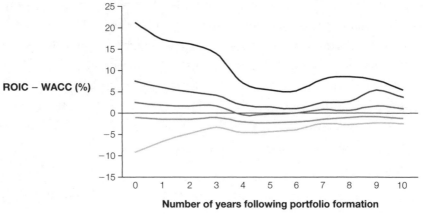

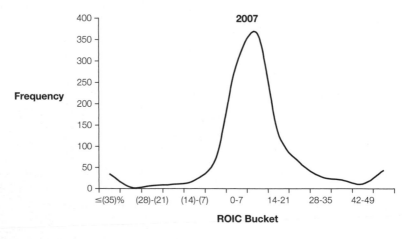

the distribution of ROICs for 2007. Note that the distribution on the top and bottom look very similar.

In contrast to Secrist's suggestion, there is no tendency for all companies to migrate toward the average or for the variance to shrink. Indeed, a different but equally valid presentation of the data shows a "movement away from mediocrity and [toward] increasing variation."[14] A more accurate view of the data is that over time, luck reshuffles the same companies and places them in different spots on the distribution. Naturally, companies that had enjoyed extreme good or bad luck will likely revert to the mean, but the overall system looks very similar through time.

What if you ran the analysis of reversion to the mean from the present to the past instead of from the past to the present? Are the parents of tall children more or less likely to be taller than their children?

A counterintuitive implication of mean reversion is that you get the same result whether you run the data forward or backward. So the parents of tall children tend to be tall, but not as tall as their children. Companies with high returns today had high returns in the past, but not as high as the present. Figure 8-5 illustrates this point by reversing the arrow of time. The quintiles are based on

FIGURE 8-5

Mean reversion also works from the present to the past (2007–1997)

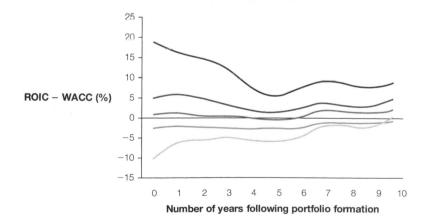

ROIC – WACC (%)

Number of years following portfolio formation

2007 ROICs—and are therefore different from the quintiles in figure 8-3—and go back to 1997. The similarity to figure 8-3 is clear.

Here's how to think about it. Say results are part persistent skill and part transitory luck. Extreme results in any given period, reflecting really good or bad luck, will tend to be less extreme either before or after that period as the contribution of luck is less significant.

What Kind of Feedback Helps Performance?

More than forty years ago, Daniel Kahneman was asked to help flight instructors in the Israeli air force sharpen their training skills. After watching the instructors hurl obscenities at the trainees, Kahneman told the instructors about research with pigeons that demonstrated how positive feedback can motivate better than castigation. One instructor retorted, "With all due respect, sir, what you're saying is for the birds." The agitated instructor went on to explain that pilots almost always did worse on their next flight after praise and consistently did better after a tongue lashing.

Initially taken aback, Kahneman soon realized that the instructor was committing our third mistake. The instructor believed that his insults caused the pilots to fly better. In reality, their performance was simply reverting to the mean. If a pilot had an unusually great flight, the instructor would be more likely to pay him a compliment. Then, as the pilot's next flight reverted to the mean, the instructor would see a more normal performance and conclude praise is bad for pilots. The instructors didn't see that their feedback was less important for the performance on the next flight than reversion to the mean.[15]

Those who thought that Steinbrenner's tantrum helped to put the Yankees in first place in 2005 made the same mistake. The main lesson is that feedback should focus on the part of the outcome a person can control. Call it the skill part, or the process. Feedback based only on outcomes is nearly useless if it fails to distinguish between skill and luck.

The Halo Effect

The halo effect, first described in the 1920s by Edward Thorndike, a psychologist at Columbia University, is closely related to reversion to the mean and illustrates a fatal flaw in much of the research for business managers. The halo effect is the human proclivity to make specific inferences based on general impressions. For example, Thorndike found that when superiors in the military rated their subordinate officers on specific qualities (e.g., intelligence, physique, leadership), the correlations among the qualities were impossibly high. If the officer liked his subordinate, he awarded generous grades across the board. If he didn't like him, he gave poor marks. In effect, the overall impression the officer made on his superior obscured the details.[16]

In *The Halo Effect,* Phil Rosenzweig showed that this mistake pervades the business world. Rosenzweig pointed out that we tend to observe financially successful companies, attach attributes (e.g., great leadership, visionary strategy, tight financial controls) to that success, and recommend that others embrace the attributes to achieve their own success. Researchers who study management often follow this formula and rarely recognize the role of luck in business performance. And the substantial data the researchers use to support their claims is all for nothing if they fall into the trap of the halo effect.[17]

For example, Rosenzweig suggests that the press will praise a company that is doing well for having "a sound strategy, a visionary leader, motivated employees, an excellent customer orientation, a vibrant culture, and so on."[18] But if the company's performance subsequently reverts to the mean, onlookers will conclude all of those features went wrong, when in reality nothing of the sort happened. In many cases, the same people are running the same business with the same strategy. Mean reversion shapes company performance, which in turn manipulates perception.

Rosenzweig offers ABB, the Swedish-Swiss industrial company, as a good example. In the mid-1990s, the *Financial Times* named

ABB the "Most Respected Company" in Europe three years in a row, suggesting the company "rated exceptionally highly for business performance, corporate strategy, and maximizing employee potential." ABB's chief executive officer, Percy Barnevik, also collected accolades. The Korean Management Association named him "the world's best honored top manager"—an award for getting the most awards.

In the late 1990s and early 2000s, ABB's performance slipped. And the same factors that the press cited as the key to ABB's success, such as agility from having decentralized management, were now the reason for the downfall, as "the far-flung units ended up causing conflicts."[19] But the press saved its largest swing in opinion for Barnevik, who went from being described as "charismatic, bold, and visionary" to "arrogant, imperial, and resistant to criticism." Richard Tomlinson and Paola Hjelt, journalists at *Fortune* magazine, reviewed ABB's highs and lows and concluded that, "Barnevik was never as good as the rave reviews he received in the 1990s, nor was he half as bad as the recent damning press coverage might suggest."[20]

While Tomlinson and Hjelt got it right, the media often perpetuates the halo effect. Successful individuals and companies adorn magazine covers, along with glowing stories explaining the secrets of their success. The halo effect also works in reverse, as the press points out the shortcomings in poor-performing companies. The press's tendency to focus on extreme performance is so predictable that it has become a reliable counter-indicator.

Tom Arnold, John Earl, and David North, finance professors at the University of Richmond, reviewed the cover stories that *Business-Week*, *Forbes*, and *Fortune* had published over a period of twenty years. They categorized the articles about companies from most bullish to most bearish. Their analysis revealed that in the two years before the cover stories were published, the stocks of the companies featured in the bullish articles had generated abnormal positive returns of more than 42 percentage points, while companies in the bearish articles underperformed by nearly 35 percentage points, consistent with what you would expect. But for the two years following the articles, the stocks of the companies that the magazines criticized outperformed the companies they praised by a margin of nearly three to one. Reversion to the mean. Sports fans have a variant of this called the *Sports Illustrated* jinx—teams or athletes tend to do worse right after they have appeared on the magazine's cover.[21]

Rosenzweig shows in devastating fashion that most of the thinking from best-selling business books falls prey to the halo effect. These books are commercially successful, he suggests, because they tell managers a story they want to hear: any company can be successful by taking these steps. In fact, no simple formula ensures success in a rapidly changing business environment.

For instance, in his widely read book *Good to Great*, Jim Collins identifies eleven great companies and notes they are all so-called hedgehogs. They focus on what they do best. They direct their efforts to doing whatever results in economic growth. And they are passionate. So one lesson of the book is that your company can succeed too, if it adopts the habits of a hedgehog. However, the important question is not, "were all great companies hedgehogs?" but rather, "were all hedgehogs great?" If the answer to the latter question is no—and it assuredly is—then dwelling on the survivors creates a bias in the analysis, leading to faulty conclusions.

Now that you are alert to the one-two punch of reversion to the mean and the halo effect, you will see it everywhere. In the late 1990s, the Corporate Executive Board did some thought-provoking research on corporate growth. I found the analysis useful and immediately integrated it into my work. About a decade later, the firm published an updated version of its analysis. At first, I was excited to get my hands on the latest findings based on "exhaustive study."

But I was soon deflated by the realization that the new work suffered from the halo effect. Unlike the prior work, the updated analysis defined a pattern of rising and falling company sales growth,

mined decades of data to find corporate performance that matched
the pattern, and then attached attributes (specific strategic, organizational, and external factors) to the companies that fit. While alluring and well packaged, the findings were based on flawed analysis.

How do you avoid mistakes associated with reversion to the
mean? Here's a checklist that may help you identify important
issues:

1. *Evaluate the mix of skill and luck in the system that you are
   analyzing.* Discerning the contributions of skill and luck is
   rarely an easy task, even if analytical tools are available.[22]
   To make the thought more concrete, consider the continuum
   of games in table 8-1. On the left are complete-information
   games, where each player knows the positions, payoffs, and
   strategies available to his opponent. In these games, the outcomes are largely settled through skill. On the right are
   games based on luck, where skill plays no role. The middle
   games combine skill and luck.

   Here's a simple test of whether an activity involves skill:
   ask if you can lose *on purpose*.[23] Think about casino games
   like roulette or slots. Winning or losing is purely a matter of
   luck. It doesn't matter what you do. But if you can lose on
   purpose, then skill is involved. This simple test reveals the
   role of luck in investing. While most people recognize that it

TABLE 8-1

What determines the outcome—skill or luck?

Skill	Skill and luck	Luck
Chess	Poker	Roulette
Checkers	Backgammon	Slot machines
Go	Monopoly	Chutes and Ladders

is hard to construct a portfolio that beats the S&P 500, most people don't know how hard it is to build a portfolio that will do a lot worse than the benchmark.

You should therefore be careful when you draw conclusions about outcomes in activities that involve luck—especially conclusions about short-term results. We're not very good at deciding how much weight to give to skill and to luck in any given situation. When something good happens, we tend to think it's because of skill. When something bad happens, we write it off to chance. So forget about the outcome and concentrate instead on the process.

Recognize, too, there is no lack of commentary about systems that are strongly influenced by chance. As the story of George Steinbrenner made us aware, luck plays an important role in baseball, especially in the short term. Yet baseball announcers analyze the games play-by-play with little awareness that luck explains most of what's going on. This same principle applies in business and markets.

2. *Carefully consider the sample size.* Daniel Kahneman and Amos Tversky established that people extrapolate unfounded conclusions from small sample sizes.[24] But thinking clearly about sample size is essential for a few reasons.

The more that luck contributes to the outcomes you observe, the larger the sample you will need to distinguish between skill and luck. Baseball is a good example. Over a 162-game season, chances are good the best teams will rise to the surface. In the short term, however, almost anything can happen. In *Moneyball,* Michael Lewis, an author who frequently provides fresh views on issues, points out, "In a five-game series, the worst team in baseball will beat the best about 15 percent of the time."[25] You do not see this in chess or tennis matches, games in which the best player almost always beats the worst, regardless of time frame.

In addition, when a large number of people participate in an activity that is influenced by chance, some of them will succeed by sheer luck. So you have to scrutinize even long, successful track records in fields with lots of participants. Investment track records are a good example.

Fans often misunderstand hot hands and streaks in games and sports. The term *hot hand* refers to the belief that success breeds success. We tend to believe that if a basketball player has made one shot, he is more likely to make the next one.

Michael Bar-Eli, a professor of business at Ben-Gurion University, studies the psychological determinants of human performance, especially as they relate to sports. With some colleagues, Bar-Eli did a detailed review of hot-hand studies, concluding tepidly that "the empirical evidence for the existence of the hot hand is considerably limited."[26]

This is not to say that players don't have streaks of made or missed shots. Naturally, they do. The point is that these strings of successes and failures are consistent with the skill level of the player. For instance, a basketball player who makes 60 percent of her shots has about a 7.8 percent chance $(0.6)^5$ of making five in a row. A player who makes 40 percent of his shots has only a 1 percent chance $(0.4)^5$ of hitting five in a row. The best players have more streaks than the worst players, just as you would expect, given the statistics.

Streaks, continuous success in a particular activity, require large doses of skill and luck. In fact, a streak is one of the best indicators of skill in a field. Luck alone can't carry a streak. My analysis of various sports streaks in basketball and baseball clearly suggests streak holders are among the most skilled in their fields.

Jerker Denrell, a professor of organizational behavior at Stanford Business School, has shown the link between the sample size and learning. In his paper, "Why Most People Disapprove of Me: Experience Sampling and Impression Formation," Denrell argues that the first impression you have of a person or organization can determine your future degree of interaction. So if you run a business that deals with customers, it is especially important to make sure that you make a favorable first impression.[27]

Imagine trying a new restaurant with two possible outcomes. In the first case, the restaurant is at its best. You have a wonderful meal with attentive service at a reasonable price. Would you go back? In the second case, the restaurant has an off day. You have a so-so dinner with indifferent service at the high end of what you had hoped to pay. Would you go back?

Most people would go back in the first case but not in the second. Given reversion to the mean, what's likely to happen the second time you go to the restaurant? Chances are the meal won't be quite as good, or the service will slip a bit. But in this case you have gathered a more accurate view of the restaurant, even if it's less flattering. On the other hand, if you never return to the restaurant because of a bad experience, you are assured you will gather no additional information, even if that information—as reversion to the mean suggests—would be more favorable. So people tend to have a better picture of people and things they like than what they don't like because they have a fuller sample.

3. *Watch for change within the system or of the system.* Not all systems remain stable over time, so it's important to consider how and why the system has changed. One obvious example is individual changes in skill level. An athlete's age is a good example. In many professional sports, athletic skill improves through the late twenties, at which point it begins to steadily deteriorate. So above-average athletes revert to the mean over time as a consequence of diminished skill. Loss of skill naturally applies to other pursuits as well, including business and medicine.

Further, the system itself may change. Stephen Jay Gould analyzed why baseball has not seen a player sustain a .400 batting average for a complete season since Ted Williams in

1941. After entertaining some possible explanations—none persuasive—Gould showed that while the mean batting average in the major leagues has been fairly stable over the years, the standard deviation has shrunk from roughly 32 percent in 1941 to about 27 percent today. The bell of the bell-shaped distribution has a narrower width than it used to. That the right side of the distribution is closer to average may explain the lack of .400 hitters. Gould attributed the reduction in standard deviation to a greater and more consistent overall skill level in the major leagues.[28]

4. *Watch out for the halo effect.* A whole cottage industry, including business school professors and consultants, is working hard to offer businesspeople tidy solutions for their problems. Here's how you grow sales. Here's how you innovate. Here's how you manage your people. But any time you see an approach offering secrets, formulas, rules, or attributes to achieve success, you can be sure that someone is selling you a nostrum. Still, spotting the halo effect requires discipline, because the purveyors are selling alluring stories and suggest substantial, albeit phony, rigor.

If you're like me and want to find a cause for every effect, you should spend some time disentangling skill from luck. An appreciation of the relative contributions of skill and luck will allow you to think clearly about reversion to the mean. To me, the greatest lesson and opportunity from understanding reversion to the mean is to keep your cool. When outcomes are really good because of a dose of good luck, prepare for the times when they will be closer to the average. When outcomes are disappointing as the result of bad luck, recognize things will get better.

Time to Think Twice

How You Can Change Your Decision Making Immediately

I ONCE ATTENDED a lecture series with a handful of colleagues. The topics, while fascinating, had a distinctly academic and abstract flavor. After the final talk, one of my coworkers sighed, "That was great, but what should I do differently tomorrow?" I'm not sure there *was* much to do differently the next day. But if the lessons of *Think Twice* have value, they suggest some very concrete actions.

Before I enumerate those actions, let's start with what you need not do. You needn't think twice before every decision. Since most decisions will be straightforward, with clear-cut repercussions, the mistakes in this book will not be relevant. We all make lots of decisions every day, and the stakes are generally low. Even when they are not low, the best course is often obvious enough.

Think Twice's value comes in situations where the stakes are sufficiently high and where your natural decision-making process leads you to a suboptimal choice.

So you must learn about the potential mistakes (prepare), identify them in context (recognize), and sharpen your ultimate decisions when the time comes (apply). Here are some thoughts on what you should do differently tomorrow.

Raise your Awareness. In the introduction, I said the mistakes had to be common, identifiable, and preventable. If my message succeeded, you will see mistakes everywhere. The first action is working to identify these mistakes in your daily stream of information. My bet is you won't lack for material.

This action is in part inspired by mathematician John Allen Paulos's books, including *A Mathematician Reads the Newspaper*.[1] Paulos entertainingly explains how looking at everyday events and commentary through the lens of a mathematician can provide a useful point of view. This is an excellent way to get comfortable with the ideas. If you can become well versed in recognizing poor thinking and second-rate decision making in others, you will be in a better position to flag a potential mistake when it faces you.

For me, the mistakes in the book trigger two reactions. On the one hand, I shake my head at the sloppy thinking all around, whether it's a case of faulty causation, the halo effect, or a failure to consider base rates. For example, while researching for this book, I found a paper that showed a correlation between the beat variances in popular songs and the standard deviation of S&P 500 index returns.[2] Naturally, the press coverage hints that the beat variance might *cause* the market moves. Possible? I guess so. Likely? I wouldn't bet my money on it.

On the other hand, the process of writing has made me even more aware of how hard it is to think clearly about a lot of problems. The reality is that we are prone to making mistakes, which when combined with incomplete information and lots of uncertainty, lead to poor outcomes. A bigger problem is what happens after the fact. Once outcomes are revealed, hindsight bias kicks in and lots of commentators suggest they knew what was going to happen before the fact. Further, when things go south, everyone wants someone to blame. (And when they go up, everyone seeks to take credit.) If nothing else, this book should encourage you to be circumspect as events and decisions unfold.

Put Yourself in the Shoes of Others. Considering the point of view or experience of other people is one of the most powerful ways to facilitate better decisions. This mind-set is vital on a number of levels. The first is embracing the outside view. While many decisions we face are rare for us—like getting married, doing a big merger deal, or moving to another community—lots of people have been through these things before. These cumulative experiences create a reference class that can guide your choices.

Thinking about the power of the situation is also essential. The idea is to be careful to avoid reading too much into the individual character of others in evaluating their choices and, rather, consider carefully the situation they are in. As we saw, the situation can help or hinder decisions to an extreme degree. Most of us, however, fall for the fundamental attribution error, incorrectly placing disposition ahead of the situation.

Keep in mind that your actions will trigger reactions, and in many cases you may not anticipate those reactions. Game theorists have been working out how best to cope with these interactions for decades, especially when they are one on one. But figuring out how a complex adaptive system will respond is also very challenging, as ecologists trying to manage an ecosystem or finance ministers trying to guide the economy will attest. Very few consequential decisions occur in a void, so you must consider the potential repercussions of any choice.[3]

Considering what motivates the decisions of others, especially when those decisions affect you, is also essential. Incentives matter. Take a negotiation course, because skilled negotiators are masters at figuring out what is important to the other party and arriving at mutually beneficial solutions. Even if you are not dealing directly with another party, understanding incentives offers valuable clues into how people decide.

Finally, leaders must develop empathy. If you are the decision maker and others live with the consequences of your choices, understanding their perspectives and feelings is the key to effectiveness. Not only will empathy help you decide, it will facilitate communication and management after the decision.

Recognize the Role of Skill and Luck. The outcomes we see in realms like business, investing, and sports are the combination of skill and luck. But most people don't do a good job of considering the relative contribution of the two. But sorting skill from luck is essential for making decisions and evaluating outcomes.

When luck is prominent in shaping outcomes, you should anticipate that reversion to the mean will make it likely that extreme outcomes are followed by more average outcomes. The bigger the part that luck plays, the more data you'll need to properly disentangle the components of skill and luck. For instance, short-term investment results largely reflect randomness and tell you little about an investor's acumen.

Finally, if you offer constructive criticism on someone else's performance, make sure you focus your comments on the skill component. This is by definition the only part of the process that an individual can control. It is too easy to conflate skill and luck in providing criticism.

Get Feedback. One of the best ways to improve decision making is through timely, accurate, and clear feedback. This type of feedback is central to deliberate practice, the essential ingredient in developing expertise. The problem is that the quality of feedback varies widely for different domains. In some realms, like weather forecasting and gambling, the feedback is quick and precise. In other fields, including long-term investing and business strategies, the feedback comes with a lag and is often ambiguous. To illustrate, research shows that weather forecasters tend to predict more accurately than financial analysts do, reflecting both the system and the feedback.[4]

The premise behind the value of feedback is that you actually want to hear it. But Philip Tetlock's in-depth study of experts reveals instead that they have "belief system defenses."[5] Even when faced with evidence that their predictions are wrong, experts conjure up ways to defend their choices, in large part to preserve their self-images. The lesson is that even good feedback is not useful if you do not use it.

If you are serious about improving your decisions and are open to feedback, there is a simple, inexpensive technique of great value—a decision-making journal. Whenever you make an important decision, take a moment to write down what you decided, how you came to that decision, and what you expect to happen. If you have the time and the inclination, you can also note how you feel physically and mentally.

A well-kept journal offers a pair of benefits. The journal allows you to audit your decisions. Too often, after we have made a decision and observed the outcome (and this is especially true for good outcomes), our minds change the story of how we decided. Having the decision-making process written in your own hand makes it much more difficult to conjure new explanations after the fact. This process of auditing is particularly useful when decisions made with a poor process lead to good outcomes.

Another benefit is the potential to find patterns. When you review your journal, you may start to see relationships between how you felt and how the decision worked out. For instance, you might note that when you are in a good mood, you are more likely to be overconfident in your assessments.

Josh Waitzkin, who has achieved world-class prominence in chess and the martial arts, describes the practice of Tigran Petrosian, a former World Chess Champion. When playing matches lasting days or weeks, Petrosian would wake up and sit quietly in his room, carefully assessing his own mood. He then built his game plan for the day based on that mood, with great success. A journal can provide a structured tool for similar introspection.[6]

Create a Checklist. When you face a tough decision, you want to be able to think clearly about what you might inadvertently overlook. That's where a decision checklist can be beneficial.

For example, in 2009 the *New England Journal of Medicine* published the results of a study tracking the rate of complications from surgery before and after the introduction of a checklist. The study was based on data from more than seventy-six hundred operations in eight cities around the world. The researchers found that rate of death dropped almost by half when the doctors used the checklist, and that other complications fell by one-third.[7] Pilots, of course, also find great value in checklists to ensure safety. But the question is whether you can develop a checklist for all activities.

People underutilize checklists. But a checklist's applicability is largely a function of a domain's stability. In stable environments, where cause and effect is pretty clear and things don't change much, checklists are great. But in rapidly changing environments that are heavily circumstantial, creating a checklist is a lot more difficult. In those environments, checklists can help with certain aspects of the decision. For instance, an investor evaluating a stock may use a checklist to make sure that she builds her financial model properly.

A good checklist balances two opposing objectives. It should be general enough to allow for varying conditions, yet specific enough to guide action. Finding this balance means a checklist should not be too long; ideally, you should be able to fit it on one or two pages.

If you have yet to create a checklist, try it and see which issues surface. Concentrate on steps or procedures, and ask where decisions have gone off track before. And recognize that errors are often the result of neglecting a step, not from executing the other steps poorly.

Perform a Premortem. Many people are familiar with a postmortem, an analysis of a decision after the outcome is known. For example, teaching hospitals hold morbidity and mortality conferences in order to review mistakes in patient care and to modify processes of decision making. But Gary Klein, a psychologist, suggests what he calls a *premortem*, a process that occurs before a decision is made. You assume you are in the future and the decision you made has failed. You then provide plausible reasons for that failure. In effect, you try to identify why your decision might lead to a poor outcome before you make the decision. Klein's research shows that premortems help people identify a greater number of potential problems than other techniques and encourage more open exchange, because no one individual or group has invested in a decision yet.

You can track your individual or group premortems in your decision journal. Watching for the possible sources of failure may also reveal early signs of trouble.[8]

Know What You Can't Know. In most day-to-day decisions, cause and effect are pretty clear. If you do X, Y will happen. But in decisions that involve systems with many interacting parts, causal links are frequently unclear. For example, what will happen with climate change? Where will terrorists strike next? When will a new technology emerge? Remember what Warren Buffett said: "Virtually all surprises are unpleasant."[9] So considering the worst-case scenarios is vital and generally overlooked in prosperous times.

Also resist the temptation to treat a complex system as if it's simpler than it is. One of the greatest challenges in finance is to create models that are useful to practitioners but also capture the market's large moves. We can trace most of the large financial disasters to a model that failed to capture the richness of outcomes inherent in a complex system like the stock market.

There's a funny paradox with decision making. Almost everyone realizes how important it is, yet very few people practice. Why don't we drill young students on decision making? How come so few professionals—executives, doctors, lawyers, and government officials—are versed in these big ideas?

There are common and identifiable mistakes that you can understand, see in your daily affairs, and manage effectively. In those cases, the correct approach to deciding well often conflicts with what your mind naturally does. But now that you know when to think twice, better decisions will follow. So prepare your mind, recognize the context, apply the right technique—and practice.

Introduction—Smart Is as Smart Does

1. Stephen Greenspan, "Why We Keep Falling for Financial Scams," *Wall Street Journal*, January 3, 2009.

2. Roger Lowenstein, *When Genius Failed: The Rise and Fall of Long-Term Capital Management* (New York: Random House, 2000).

3. Laurence Gonzales, *Everyday Survival: Why Smart People Do Stupid Things* (New York: W.W. Norton & Company, 2008), 92–97.

4. Camilla Anderson, "Iceland Gets Help to Recover from Historic Crisis," *IMF Survey Online*, December 2, 2008; and Michael Lewis, "Wall Street on the Tundra," *Vanity Fair*, April 2009, 140–147, 173–177.

5. Keith E. Stanovich, *What Intelligence Tests Miss: The Psychology of Rational Thought* (New Haven, CT: Yale University Press, 2009), 2–3.

6. Richard H. Thaler, "Anomalies: The Winner's Curse," *The Journal of Economic Perspectives* 2, no. 1 (1988): 191–202.

7. Max H. Bazerman, *Judgment in Managerial Decision Making*, 6th ed. (New York: John Wiley & Sons, 2006), 33–35.

8. Rosemarie Nagel, "Unraveling in Guessing Games: An Experimental Study," *American Economic Review* 85, no. 5 (1995): 1313–1326. Also, Richard H. Thaler, "From Homo Economicus to Homo Sapiens," *The Journal of Economic Perspectives* 14, no. 1 (2000): 133–141. I have run this experiment in my own class for years. In descending order, the most popular responses are 0, 22, 1, and 33. For more details on why people stop at between one to two levels of deduction, see Colin F. Camerer, Teck-Hua Ho, and Juin-Kuan Chong, "A Cognitive Hierarchy Model of Games," *The Quarterly Journal of Economics* 119, no. 3 (2004): 861–898.

9. Scott E. Page, *The Difference: How the Power of Diversity Creates Better Groups, Firms, Schools, and Societies* (Princeton, NJ: Princeton University Press, 2007), 36–41.

10. J. Edward Russo and Paul J. H. Schoemaker, *Winning Decisions: Getting It Right the First Time* (New York: Doubleday, 2002), 9 and 124.

11. Nassim Nicholas Taleb, *Fooled by Randomness: The Hidden Role of Chance in Life and in the Markets*, 2nd ed. (New York: Thomson Texere, 2004).

12. Daniel Kahneman and Amos Tversky, "Prospect Theory: An Analysis of Decision Making Under Risk," *Econmetrica* 47, no. 2 (1979): 263–291.

13. Danny Kahneman, "A Short Course in Thinking about Thinking," *Edge.org*, 2007, http://www.edge.org/3rd_culture/kahneman07/kahneman07_index.html.

Chapter 1—The Outside View: Why Big Brown Was a Bad Bet

1. Tom Pedulla, "Big Brown Makes His Run at Immortality," *USA Today*, June 6, 2008.

2. Ryan O'Halloran, "A 'Foregone Conclusion'?" *Washington Times*, May 30, 2008.

3. Technically, Big Brown did not finish last. His jockey eased him. Record keepers list an eased horse last in the chart, but the horse is not considered a finisher.

4. Arthur Bloch, *Murphy's Law: The 26th Anniversary Edition* (New York: Perigee Trade, 2003), 70–71.

5. I got these statistics from *Cristblog with Steve Crist*, including "Triple Crown Bids" (May 19, 2008) and "Triple Crown Figs" (May 21, 2008). See http:// cristblog.drf.com/.

6. Dan Lovallo and Daniel Kahneman, "Delusions of Success," *Harvard Business Review*, July 2003, 56–63.

7. Shelley E. Taylor and Jonathan D. Brown, "Illusion and Well-Being: A Social Psychological Perspective on Mental Health," *Psychological Bulletin* 103, no. 2 (1988): 193–210.

8. Mark D. Alicke and Olesya Govorun, "The Better-Than-Average Effect," in *The Self in Social Judgment*, ed. Mark D. Alicke, David A. Dunning, and Joachim I. Krueger (New York: Psychology Press, 2005), 85–106.

9. Justin Kruger and David Dunning, "Unskilled and Unaware of It: How Difficulties in Recognizing One's Own Incompetence Lead to Inflated Self-Assessments," *Journal of Personality and Social Psychology* 77, no. 6 (1999): 1121–1134.

10. Neil D. Weinstein, "Unrealistic Optimism about Future Life Events," *Journal of Personality and Social Psychology* 39, no. 5 (1980): 806–820.

11. Ellen J. Langer, "The Illusion of Control," *Journal of Personality and Social Psychology* 32, no. 2 (1975): 311–328.

12. Michael C. Jensen, "The Performance of Mutual Funds in the Period 1945–1964," *The Journal of Finance* 23, no. 2 (1968): 389–416. Also, Burton G. Malkiel, "Returns from Investing in Equity Mutual Funds 1971–1991," *The Journal of Finance* 50, no. 2 (1995): 549–572. For the paucity of funds that outperform due to skill, see Laurent Barras, O. Scaillet, and Russ R. Wermers, "False Discoveries in Mutual Fund Performance: Measuring Luck in Estimated Alphas," Robert H. Smith School research paper RH 06-043, Swiss Finance Institute research paper 08-18, September 1, 2008. For the quantification of the cost of active management, see Kenneth R. French, "Presidential Address: The Cost of Active Investing," *The Journal of Finance* 63, no. 4 (2008): 1537–1573.

13. Mark L. Sirower, *The Synergy Trap: How Companies Lose the Acquisition Game* (New York: Free Press, 1997), 123; Tom Copeland, Tim Koller, and Jack Murrin, *Valuation: Measuring and Managing the Value of Companies*, 3rd ed. (New York: John Wiley & Sons, 2000), 114–115.

14. Francesco Guerrera and Julie MacIntosh, "Luck Played Part in Rohm and Haas Deal," *Financial Times*, July 10, 2008.

15. Alfred Rappaport and Michael J. Mauboussin, *Expectations Investing: Reading Stock Prices for Better Returns* (Boston: Harvard Business School Press, 2001), 153–169.

16. For the evolution in patient-physician model, see Raisa B. Deber, "Physicians in Health Care Management: The Patient-Physician Partnership: Decision Making, Problem Solving and the Desire to Participate," *Canadian Medical Association* 151, no. 4 (1994): 423–427. For poor decisions, see Donald A. Redelmeier, Paul Rozin, and Daniel Kahneman, "Understanding Patients' Decisions: Cognitive and Emotional Perspectives," *The Journal of the American Medical Association* 270, no. 1 (1993): 72–76.

17. Angela K. Freymuth and George F. Ronan, "Modeling Patient Decision-Making: The Role of Base-Rate and Anecdotal Information," *Journal of Clinical Psychology in Medical Settings* 11, no. 3 (2004): 211–216. For more on the power of stories, see Mark Turner, *The Literary Mind* (New York: Oxford University Press, 1996).

18. Roger Buehler, Dale Griffin, and Michael Ross, "Inside the Planning Fallacy: The Causes and Consequences of Optimistic Time Predictions," in *Heuristics and Biases: The Psychology of Intuitive Judgment*, ed. Thomas Gilovich, Dale Griffin, and Daniel Kahneman (Cambridge: Cambridge University Press, 2002), 250–270.

19. Daniel Gilbert, *Stumbling on Happiness* (New York: Alfred A. Knopf, 2006), 228. Also, see James G. March, *A Primer on Decision Making: How Decisions Happen* (New York: Free Press, 1994).

20. Danny Kahneman, "A Short Course in Thinking about Thinking," *Edge.org,* 2007. For great examples of the failure of outside thinking in sports, see Michael Lewis, *Moneyball: The Art of Winning an Unfair Game* (New York: WW Norton & Company, 2003); and David Romer, "Do Firms Maximize? Evidence from Professional Football," *The Journal of Political Economy* 114, no. 2 (2006): 340–365.

21. Daniel Kahneman and Amos Tversky, "Intuitive Prediction: Biases and Corrective Procedures," in *Judgment Under Uncertainty: Heuristics and Biases*, ed. Daniel Kahneman, Paul Slovic, and Amos Tversky (Cambridge: Cambridge University Press, 1982), 414–421. For a simplified version, see Lovallo and Kahneman, "Delusions of Success."

22. Stephen Jay Gould, *Full House: The Spread of Excellence from Plato to Darwin* (New York: Harmony Books, 1996), 45–56.

23. Chuck Bower and Frank Frigo, "What Was Coach Thinking?" *New York Times*, February 1, 2009.

Chapter 2—Open to Options: How Your Telephone Number Can Influence Your Decisions

1. Steven Schultz, "Freshman Learn About Thinking from Nobel Laureate," *Princeton Weekly Bulletin* 94, no. 3 (2004).

2. Amos Tversky and Daniel Kahneman, "Judgment under Uncertainty: Heuristics and Biases," *Science* 185, no. 4157 (1974): 1124–1131.

3. Philip Johnson-Laird, *How We Reason* (Oxford: Oxford University Press, 2006), 417.

4. Billy Goodman, "Thinking about Thinking," *Princeton Alumni Weekly*, January 29, 2003, 26–27.

5. Philip N. Johnson-Laird, *Mental Models* (Cambridge: Harvard University Press, 1983); for a less formal discussion, see Peter D. Kaufman, ed., *Poor Charlie's Almanack,* 2nd ed. (Virginia Beach, VA: PCA Publication, 2006). See also, Laurence Gonzales, *Everyday Survival: Why Smart People Do Stupid Things* (New York: W.W. Norton & Company, 2008), 19–32.

6. To be more formal, the mental-models theory makes three assumptions. First, each model represents a possibility, capturing most of the common ways the possibility can occur. Second, the models are "iconic"; the parts of the model correspond to what it represents. And, finally, mental models represent what is true but do not represent what is false. See Philip N. Johnson-Laird, "Mental Models and Reasoning," in *The Nature of Reasoning*, ed. Jacqueline P. Leighton and Robert J. Sternberg (Cambridge: Cambridge University Press, 2004), 169–204.

7. Nicholas Epley and Thomas Gilovich, "The Anchoring-and-Adjustment Heuristic: Why the Adjustments Are Insufficient," *Psychological Science* 17, no. 4 (2006): 311–318.

8. Gregory B. Northcraft and Margaret A. Neale, "Experts, Amateurs, and Real Estate: An Anchoring-and-Adjustment Perspective on Property Pricing Decisions," *Organizational Behavior and Human Decision Processes* 39, no. 1 (1987): 84–97.

9. Adam D. Galinsky and Thomas Mussweiler, "First Offers as Anchors: The Role of Perspective-Taking and Negotiator Focus," *Journal of Personality and Social Psychology* 81, no. 4 (2001): 657–669. See also, Deepak Malhotra and Max H. Bazerman, *Negotiation Genius: How to Overcome Obstacles and Achieve Brilliant Results at the Bargaining Table and Beyond* (New York: Bantam Books, 2007), 27–42.

10. Jerome Groopman, *How Doctors Think* (Boston: Houghton Mifflin, 2007), 41–44.

11. Ibid., 63–64; and Ian Ayres, *Super Crunchers: Why Thinking-by-Numbers is the New Way to be Smart* (New York: Bantam Books, 2007), 98–99.

12. Jason Zweig, *Your Money and Your Brain: How the New Science of Neuroeconomics Can Help Make You Rich* (New York: Simon & Schuster, 2007), 53–84.

13. Scott A. Huettel, Peter B. Mack, and Gregory McCarthy, "Perceiving Patterns in Random Series: Dynamic Processing of Sequence in Prefrontal Cortex," *Nature Neuroscience* 5, no. 5 (2002): 485–490.

14. Leeat Yariv, "I'll See It When I Believe It—A Simple Model of Cognitive Consistency," discussion paper 1352, Cowles Foundation, New Haven, CT, February 2002.

15. Carol Tavris and Elliot Aronson, *Mistakes Were Made (but not by* me*): Why We Justify Foolish Beliefs, Bad Decisions, and Hurtful Acts* (Orlando, FL: Harcourt, Inc., 2007), 13.

16. John F. Ashton, *In Six Days: Why Fifty Scientists Choose to Believe in Creation* (Green Forest, AZ: Master Books, 2001), 351–355; Richard Dawkins, *The God Delusion* (Boston: Houghton Mifflin Company, 2006), 284–286.

17. Leon Festinger, Henry W. Riecken, and Stanley Schachter, *When Prophecy Fails: A Social and Psychological Study of a Modern Group That Predicted the Destruction of the World* (Minneapolis: University of Minnesota Press, 1956), 168.

18. Ibid., 176.

19. Raymond S. Nickerson, "Confirmation Bias: A Ubiquitous Phenomenon in Many Guises," *Review of General Psychology* 2, no. 2 (1998): 175–220.

20. Robert B. Cialdini, *Influence: The Psychology of Persuasion,* rev. ed. (New York: Quill, 1993),60–61.

21. Elihu Katz and Paul F. Lazarsfeld, *Personal Influence: The Part Played by People in the Flow of Mass Communications* (New York: Free Press, 1955).

22. See http://www.thesmokinggun.com/archive/0322061cheney1.html.

23. Drew Westen, Pavel S. Blagov, Keith Harenski, Clint Kilts, and Stephan Hamann, "Neural Bases of Motivated Reasoning: An fMRI Study of Emotional Constraints on Partisan Political Judgment in the 2004 U.S. Presidential Election," *Journal of Cognitive Neuroscience* 18, no. 11 (2006): 1947–1958.

24. "Political Bias Affects Brain Activity, Study Finds," *MSNBC.com*, January 24, 2006.

25. Marvin M. Chun and René Marois, "The Dark Side of Visual Attention," *Current Opinion in Neurobiology* 12, no. 2 (2002): 184–189; Daniel J. Simons and Christopher F. Chabris, "Gorillas in Our Midst: Sustained Inattentional Blindness for Dynamic Events," *Perception* 28, no. 9 (1999): 1059–1074; William James, *The Principles of Psychology*, vol. 1 (New York: Henry Holt & Co., 1890); Richard Wiseman, *Did You Spot the Gorilla? How to Recognize Hidden Opportunities* (London: Random House, 2004); Arien Mack and Irvin Rock, *Inattentional Blindness* (Cambridge: MIT Press, 1998); and Torkel Klingberg, *The Overflowing Brain: Information Overload and the Limits of Working Knowledge* (New York: Oxford University Press, 2009).

26. David Klinger, *Into the Kill Zone: A Cop's Eye View of Deadly Force* (San Francisco: Jossey-Bass, 2004).

27. Robert M. Sapolsky, *Why Zebras Don't Get Ulcers: An Updated Guide to Stress, Stress-Related Disease, and Coping* (New York: W.H. Freeman and Company, 1994); and Samuel M. McClure, David I Laibson, George Loewsenstein, and Jonathan D. Cohen, "Separate Neural Systems Value Immediate and Delayed Monetary Rewards," *Science* 306 (October 15, 2004), 503–507.

28. Jerome Groopman tells a similar story. See Groopman, *How Doctors Think*, 225–233.

29. George A. Akerlof and Robert J. Shiller, *Animal Spirits: How Human Psychology Drives the Economy, and Why It Matters for Global Capitalism* (Princeton, NJ: Princeton University Press, 2009), 36–37; and Whitney Tilson and Glenn Tongue, *More Mortgage Meltdown: 6 Ways to Profit in These Bad Times* (New York: John Wiley & Sons, 2009), 29–47.

30. Alan Greenspan, "Testimony to the Committee of Government Oversight and Reform," October 23, 2008.

31. Max H. Bazerman, George Loewenstein, and Don A. Moore, "Why Good Accountants Do Bad Audits," *Harvard Business Review,* November 2002, 97–102; and Don A. Moore, Philip E. Tetlock, Lloyd Tanlu, and Max H. Bazerman, "Conflicts of Interest and the Case of Auditor Independence: Moral Seduction and Strategic Issue Cycling," *Academy of Management Review* 31, no. 1 (2006): 10–29.

32. Malhotra and Bazerman, *Negotiation Genius*, 19–24. See also, Max H. Bazerman and Michael D. Watkins, *Predictable Surprises: The Disasters You*

Should Have Seen Coming and How to Prevent Them (Boston: Harvard Business School Press, 2004).

33. J. Edward Russo and Paul J. H. Schoemaker, *Winning Decisions: Getting It Right the First Time* (New York: Currency, 2002), 86–89.

34. Doris Kearns Goodwin, *Team of Rivals: The Political Genius of Abraham Lincoln* (New York: Simon & Schuster, 2005).

35. Søren Kierkegaard, *The Diary of Søren Kierkegaard* (New York: Carol Publishing Group, 1993), 111; and Max H. Bazerman, *Judgment in Managerial Decision Making,* 6th ed. (New York: John Wiley & Sons, 2006), 37–39.

36. Antonio Damasio, *The Feeling of What Happens: Body and Emotion in the Making of Consciousness* (New York: Harcourt Brace & Company, 1999), 42.

Chapter 3—The Expert Squeeze: Why Netflix Knows More Than Clerks Do About Your Favorite Films

1. James Surowiecki, *The Wisdom of Crowds: Why the Many Are Smarter Than the Few and How Collective Wisdom Shapes Business, Economies, Societies and Nations* (New York: Doubleday and Company, 2004).

2. Gary Hamel with Bill Breen, *The Future of Management* (Boston: Harvard Business School Press, 2007), 229–239; Renée Dye, "The Promise of Prediction Markets: A Roundtable," *The McKinsey Quarterly,* no. 2 (April 2008): 83–93; and Steve Lohr, "Betting to Improve the Odds," *New York Times,* April 9, 2008.

3. Prediction markets are real-money exchanges where people can bet on events with binary and temporally defined outcomes; hence the price reflects the probability of the event occurring. See Kenneth J. Arrow, Robert Forsythe, Michael Gorham, Robert Hahn, Robin Hansen, John O. Ledyard, Saul Levmore, Robert Litan, Paul Milgrom, Forrest D. Nelson, George R. Neumann, Marco Ottaviani, Thomas C. Schelling, Robert J. Shiller, Vernon L. Smith, Erik Snowberg, Cass R. Sunstein, Paul C. Tetlock, Philip E. Tetlock, Hal R. Varian, Justin Wolfers, and Eric Zitzewitz, "The Promise of Prediction Markets," *Science* 320 (May 16, 2008):877–878; Bo Cowgill, Justin Wolfers, and Eric Zitzewitz, "Using Prediction Markets to Track Information Flows: Evidence from Google," working paper, 2008.

4. Phred Dvorak, "Best Buy Taps 'Prediction Market,'" *Wall Street Journal,* September 16, 2008.

5. Hilke Plassmann, John O'Doherty, Baba Shiv, and Antonio Rangel, "Marketing Actions Can Modulate Neural Representations of Experienced Pleasantness," *Proceedings of the National Academy of Sciences* 105, no. 3 (2008): 1050–1054.

6. Ian Ayres, *Super Crunchers: Why Thinking-by-Numbers Is the New Way to Be Smart* (New York: Bantam Books, 2007), 1–6. Actually, this is not the formula Ayres shows. A check of primary sources suggests Ayres made two errors in his equation (the constant should be a negative value and a decimal place is off). I believe this equation is correct.

7. Orley Ashenfelter, "Predicting the Quality and Prices of Bordeaux Wines," Working paper no. 4, American Association of Wine Economists, April 2007.

8. Steven Pinker, *How the Mind Works* (New York: W.W Norton & Company, 1997), 305–306.

9. J. Scott Armstrong, Monica Adya, and Fred Collopy, "Rule-Based Forecasting: Using Judgment in Time-Series Extrapolation" in *Principles of Forecasting: A Handbook for Researchers and Practitioners,* ed. J. Scott Armstrong (New York: Springer, 2001), 259–282; and John D. Sterman and Linda Booth Sweeney, "Managing Complex Dynamic Systems: Challenge and Opportunity for Naturalistic Decision-Making Theory," in *How Professionals Make Decisions,* ed. Henry Montgomery, Raanan Lipshitz, and Berndt Brehmer (Mahway, NJ: Lawrence Erlbaum Associates, 2005), 57–90.

10. Gary Loveman, "Diamonds in the Data Mine," *Harvard Business Review,* May 2003, 109–113.

11. Michael T. Belongia, "Predicting Interest Rates: A Comparison of Professional and Market-Based Forecasts," *Federal Reserve Bank of St. Louis,* March 1987, 9–15; and Deirdre N. McCloskey, *If You're So Smart: The Narrative of Economic Expertise* (Chicago: University of Chicago Press, 1990), 111–122.

12. Joe Nocera, "On Oil Supply, Opinions Aren't Scarce," *New York Times,* September 10, 2005.

13. Eric Bonabeau, "Don't Trust Your Gut," *Harvard Business Review,* May 2003, 116–123.

14. Michael J. Mauboussin, "What Good Are Experts?" *Harvard Business Review,* February 2008, 43–44; and Bruce G. Buchanan, Randall Davis, and Edward A. Feigenbaum, "Expert Systems: A Perspective from Computer Science" in *The Cambridge Handbook of Expertise and Expert Performance,* ed. K. Anders Ericsson, Neil Charness, Paul J. Feltovich, and Robert R. Hoffman (Cambridge: Cambridge University Press, 2006), 87–103.

15. For more on the contest, see www.netflixprize.com. Clive Thompson, "If You Liked This, You're Sure to Love That," *New York Times Magazine,* November 23, 2008. Jordan Ellenberg, "The Netflix Challenge: This Psychologist Might Outsmart the Math Brains Competing for the Netflix Prize," *Wired Magazine,* March 2008, 114–122.

16. Paul E. Meehl, *Clinical versus Statistical Prediction: A Theoretical Analysis and a Review of the Evidence* (Minneapolis: University of Minnesota Press, 1954); Robyn M. Dawes, David Faust, and Paul E. Meehl, "Clinical versus Actuarial Judgment," in *Heuristics and Biases: The Psychology of Intuitive Judgment,* ed. Thomas Gilovich, Dale Griffin, and Daniel Kahneman (Cambridge: Cambridge University Press, 2002), 716–729; Reid Hastie and Robyn M. Dawes, *Rational Choice in an Uncertain World* (Thousand Oaks, CA: Sage Publications, 2001), 55–72; and William M. Grove, David H. Zald, Boyd S. Lebow, Beth E. Snitz, and Chad Nelson, "Clinical Versus Mechanical Prediction: A Meta-Analysis," *Psychological Assessment* 12, no. 1 (2000): 19–30.

17. Philip E. Tetlock, *Expert Political Judgment: How Good Is It? How Can We Know?* (Princeton, NJ: Princeton University Press, 2005), 54.

18. Scott E. Page, *The Difference: How the Power of Diversity Creates Better Groups, Firms, Schools, and Societies* (Princeton, NJ: Princeton University Press, 2007), 205–214. Crowds solve different types of problems. See Michael J. Mauboussin, "Explaining the Wisdom of Crowds: Applying the Logic of Diversity," *Mauboussin on Strategy,* March 20, 2007.

19. In his classic paper on market efficiency, Jack Treynor suggests the accuracy of the average guess "comes from the faulty opinions of a large

number of investors who err independently. If their errors are wholly independent, the standard error in equilibrium price declines with roughly the square root of the number of investors." I believe the square-root law, which says the standard error of the mean decreases with the square root of N (number of observations), is an inappropriate explanation for the jellybean (or broader wisdom of crowds) problem. The square-root law applies to sampling theory, where there are independent observations that include the answer plus a random noise term. Over a large number of observations, the errors cancel out. The underlying assumption behind the square-root law is that observations are independent and identically distributed around a mean. This is clearly not the case in many instances. While the diversity prediction theorem allows for the square-root law, it does not require it. I believe the diversity prediction theorem is a more robust way to explain the wisdom of crowds. See Jack L. Treynor, "Market Efficiency and the Bean Jar Experiment," *Financial Analysts Journal*, May–June 1987, 50–53.

20. J. Scott Armstrong, "Combining Forecasts," in *Principles of Forecasting: A Handbook for Researchers and Practitioners,* ed. J. Scott Armstrong (New York: Springer, 2001), 417–439.

21. Malcolm Gladwell, *Blink: The Power of Thinking Without Thinking* (New York: Little, Brown and Company, 2005); and Gary Klein, *Sources of Power: How People Make Decisions* (Cambridge: MIT Press, 1998).

22. Daniel Kahneman, "Maps of Bounded Rationality: A Perspective on Intuitive Judgment and Choice," Nobel Prize Lecture, December 8, 2002, Stockholm, Sweden.

23. Michelene T. H. Chi, Robert Glaser, and Marshall Farr, eds., *The Nature of Expertise* (Hillsdale, NJ: Lawrence Erlbaum Associates, 1988), xvii–xx; Robin M. Hogarth, *Educating Intuition* (Chicago: University of Chicago Press, 2001); David G. Myers, *Intuition: Its Powers and Perils* (New Haven, CT: Yale University Press, 2002); Gerd Gigerenzer, *Gut Feelings: The Intelligence of the Unconscious* (New York: Viking, 2007); and Charles M. Abernathy and Robert M. Hamm, *Surgical Intuition: What It Is and How to Get It* (Philadelphia: Hanley & Belfus, 1995).

24. Geoff Colvin, *Talent is Overrated: What* Really *Separates World-Class Performers from Everybody Else* (New York: Portfolio 2008), 65–72.

25. Malcolm Gladwell, "Reinventing Invention," speech at *The New Yorker* Conference, May 8, 2008. See http://www.newyorker.com/online/video/conference/ 2008/gladwell; see also, Malcolm Gladwell, "Most Likely to Succeed: How Do We Hire When We Can't Tell Who's Right for the Job?" *The New Yorker*, December 15, 2008, 36–42.

26. Frank E. Kuzmits and Arthur J. Adams, "The NFL Combine: Does It Predict Performance in the National Football League?" *The Journal of Strength and Conditioning Research* 22, no. 6 (2008): 1721–1727.

27. Duncan J. Watts, "A Simple Model of Global Cascades on Random Networks," Proceedings of the National Academy of Sciences 99, no. 9, April 30, 2002: 5766–5771; Duncan J. Watts, *Six Degrees: The Science of a Connect Age* (New York: W.W. Norton & Company, 2003); and Victor M. Eguiluz and Martin G. Zimmerman, "Transmission of Information and Herd Behavior: An Application to Financial Markets," *Physical Review Letters* 85, no. 26 (2000): 5659–5662.

28. Irving Janis, *Groupthink: Psychological Studies of Policy Decisions and Fiascoes*, 2nd ed. (Boston: Houghton Mifflin, 1982); and Cass R. Sunstein, *Infotopia: How Many Minds Produce Knowledge* (Oxford: Oxford University Press, 2006), 45–46.

29. Tetlock, *Expert Political Judgment*, 73–75.

30. Saul Hansell, "Google Answer to Filling Jobs Is an Algorithm," *New York Times*, January 3, 2007.

Chapter 4—Situational Awareness: How Accordion Music Boosts Sales of Burgundy

1. S. E. Asch, "Effects of Group Pressure Upon the Modification and Distortion of Judgments," in *Groups, Leadership and Men,* ed. Harold Guetzkow (Pittsburgh: Carnegie Press, 1951), 177–190.

2. Gregory S. Berns, Jonathan Chappelow, Caroline F. Zink, Giuseppe Pagnoni, Megan Martin-Skurski, and Jim Richards, "Neurobiological Correlates of Social Conformity and Independence During Mental Rotation," *Biological Psychiatry* 58 (22 June 2005): 245–253.

3. Sandra Blakeslee, "What Other People Say May Change What You See," *New York Times*, June 28, 2005.

4. Gregory Berns, *Iconoclast: A Neuroscientist Reveals How to Think Differently* (Boston: Harvard Business Press, 2008), 92–97.

5. "Conformity," *ABC Primetime Lab*, January 12, 2006. See http://abcnews. go.com/Primetime/Health/story?id=1495038.

6. Paul Slovic, Melissa Finucane, Ellen Peters, and Donald G. MacGregor, "The Affect Heuristic," in *Heuristics and Biases: The Psychology of Intuitive Judgment,* ed. Thomas Gilovich, Dale Griffin, and Daniel Kahneman (Cambridge: Cambridge University Press, 2002), 397–420.

7. David Berreby, *Us and Them: Understanding Your Tribal Mind* (New York: Little, Brown and Company, 2005).

8. Lee Ross, "The Intuitive Psychologist and His Shortcomings," in *Advances in Experimental Social Psychology,* ed. Leonard Berkowitz (New York: Academic Press, 1977), 173–220; and Thomas Gilovich, Dacher Keltner, and Richard E. Nisbett, *Social Psychology* (New York: W.W. Norton & Company, 2006), 360–369.

9. Richard E. Nisbett, *The Geography of Thought: How Asians and Westerners Think Differently . . . and Why* (New York: Free Press, 2003).

10. Michael W. Morris and Kaiping Peng, "Culture and Cause: American and Chinese Attributions for Social and Physical Events," *Journal of Personality and Social Psychology* 67, no. 6 (1994): 949–971.

11. Adrian C. North, David J. Hargreaves, and Jennifer McKendrick, "In-store Music Affects Product Choice," *Nature* 390 (November 13, 2007): 13.

12. John A. Bargh, Mark Chen, and Laura Burrows, "Automaticity of Social Behavior: Direct Effects of Trait Construction and Stereotype Activation on Action," *Journal of Personality and Social Psychology* 71, no. 2, (1996): 230–244.

13. Ibid.

14. Rob W. Holland, Merel Hendriks, and Henk Aarts, "Smells Like Clean Spirit: Nonconscious Effects of Scent on Cognition and Behavior," *Psychological Science* 16, no. 9 (2005): 689–693.

15. Naomi Mandel and Eric J. Johnson, "When Web Pages Influence Choice: Effects of Visual Primes on Experts and Novices," *Journal of Consumer Research* 29, no. 2 (2002): 235–245.

16. Eric J. Johnson and Daniel Goldstein, "Do Defaults Save Lives?" *Science* 302 (November 21, 2003): 1338–1339.

17. Richard H. Thaler and Cass R. Sunstein, *Nudge: Improving Decisions About Health, Wealth, and Happiness* (New Haven, CT: Yale University Press, 2008); Daniel G. Goldstein, Eric J. Johnson, Andreas Herrmann, and Mark Heitmann, "Nudge Your Customers Toward Better Choices," *Harvard Business Review*, December 2008, 99–105; and Dan Ariely, *Predictably Irrational: The Hidden Forces That Shape Our Decisions* (New York: Harper, 2008), 1–6.

18. George F. Loewenstein, Elke U. Weber, Christopher K. Hsee, and Ned Welch, "Risk as Feelings," *Psychological Bulletin* 127, no. 2 (2001): 267–286.

19. R. B. Zajonc, ed., *The Selected Works of R. B. Zajonc* (New York: John Wiley & Sons, 2004), 256.

20. For example, after good returns in the stock market, investors expect continued outsized returns. See Donald G. MacGregor, "Imagery and Financial Judgment," *The Journal of Psychology and Financial Markets* 3, no. 1 (2002): 15–22.

21. Slovic et al., "The Affect Heuristic," 408.

22. Stanley Milgram, *Obedience to Authority* (New York: Harper & Row, 1974), 6.

23. Jerry M. Burger, "Replicating Milgram: Would People Still Obey Today?" *American Psychologist* 64, no. 1 (2009): 1–11.

24. Philip Zimbardo, *The Lucifer Effect: Understanding How Good People Turn Evil* (New York: Random House, 2007).

25. Ibid., 210–221.

26. Peter F. Drucker, *Management Challenges for the 21st Century* (New York: HarperBusiness, 1999), 74.

27. David Leonhardt, "Why Doctors So Often Get It Wrong," *New York Times,* February 22, 2006.

28. Atul Gawande, "The Checklist," *The New Yorker*, December 10, 2007, 86–95; Atul Gawande, "A Lifesaving Checklist," *New York Times*, December 30, 2007; and Peter Pronovost, "Testimony before Government Oversight Committee," April 16, 2008.

29. Bargh, Chen, and Burrows, "Automaticity of Social Behavior," 241.

30. Zimbardo, *The Lucifer Effect,* 451–456.

31. Warren E. Buffett, "Chairman's Letter," *Berkshire Hathaway Annual Report to Shareholders*, 1989.

32. Michiyo Nakamoto and David Wighton, "Citigroup Chief Stays Bullish on Buy-Outs," *Financial Times,* July 9, 2007.

Chapter 5—More Is Different: How Bees Find the Best Hive Without a Real Estate Agent

1. Quote from biologist Deborah Gordon in Peter Miller, "The Genius of Swarms," *National Geographic*, July 2007, 126–147. See also Herbert A. Simon, *The Sciences of the Artificial*, 3rd ed. (Cambridge: MIT Press, 1996), 51–54.

2. Thomas D. Seeley, P. Kirk Visscher, and Kevin M. Passino, "Group Decision Making in Honey Bee Swarms," *American Scientist* 94, no. 3 (2006): 220–229.

3. For a popular treatment, see Eric Bonabeau and Guy Théraulaz, "Swarm Smarts," *Scientific American*, March 2000, 82–90. See also Eric Bonabeau, Marco Dorigo, and Guy Théraulaz, *Swarm Intelligence: From Natural to Artificial Systems* (New York: Oxford University Press, 1999); Thomas D. Seeley, *The Wisdom of the Hive* (Cambridge: Harvard University Press, 1995); and Steven Johnson, *Emergence: The Connected Lives of Ants, Brains, Cities, and Software* (New York: Scribner, 2001).

4. Thomas D. Seeley and P. Kirk Visscher, "Sensory Coding of Nest-site Value in Honeybee Swarms," *The Journal of Experimental Biology* 211, no. 23 (2008): 3691–3697.

5. See John H. Holland, *Hidden Order: How Adaptation Builds Complexity* (Reading, MA: Helix Books, 1995); Murray Gell-Mann, *The Quark and the Jaguar: Adventures in the Simple and the Complex* (New York: W.H. Freeman, 1994); and John H. Miller and Scott E. Page, *Complex Adaptive Systems: An Introduction to Computational Models of Social Life* (Princeton, NJ: Princeton University Press, 2007).

6. P. W. Anderson, "More is Different," *Science* 177, no. 4047 (1972): 393–396. See also Herbert A. Simon, "The Architecture of Complexity," *Proceedings of the American Philosophical Society* 106, no. 6 (1962): 467–482; and Thomas C. Schelling, *Micromotives and Macrobehavior* (New York: W.W. Norton & Company, 1978).

7. Lewis Wolpert, *Six Impossible Things Before Breakfast: The Evolutionary Origins of Belief* (New York: W.W. Norton, 2007). See also Gilles Fauconnier and Mark Turner, *The Way We Think: Conceptual Blending and the Mind's Hidden Complexities* (New York: Basic Books, 2002), 75–87.

8. Joseph LeDoux, *The Emotional Brain: The Mysterious Underpinnings of Emotional Life* (New York: Touchstone, 1996), 32–33. See also David M. Cutler, James M. Poterba, and Lawrence H. Summers, "What Moves Stock Prices?" *The Journal of Portfolio Management*, Spring 1989, 4–12.

9. Shyam Sunder, "Relationship Between Accounting Changes and Stock Prices: Problems of Measurement and Some Empirical Evidence," *Journal of Accounting Research: Empirical Research in Accounting: Selected Studies 1973* 11 (1973): 1–45.

10. Vernon L. Smith, *Rationality in Economics: Constructivist and Ecological Forms* (Cambridge: Cambridge University Press, 2008). See also Charles R. Plott and Vernon L. Smith, eds., *Handbook of Experimental Economics Results: Volume 1* (Amsterdam: North-Holland, 2008).

11. John R. Graham, Campbell R. Harvey, and Shiva Rajgopal, "Value Destruction and Financial Reporting Decisions," *Financial Analysts Journal* 62, no. 6 (2006): 27–39.

12. This is a bias that arises from the availability heuristic. See Max H. Bazerman, *Judgment in Managerial Decision Making*, 6th ed. (New York: John Wiley & Sons, 2006), 18–21.

13. Alston Chase, *Playing God in Yellowstone: The Destruction of America's First National Park* (Boston: The Atlantic Monthly Press, 1986). See also Douglas W. Smith and Gary Ferguson, *Decade of the Wolf: Returning the Wild to Yellowstone* (Guilford, CT: The Lyons Press, 2005).

14. Chase, *Playing God in Yellowstone*, 44.

15. Robert K. Merton, "The Unanticipated Consequences of Purposive Social Action," *American Sociological Review* 1, no. 6 (1936): 894–904.

16. James Surowiecki, "Did Lehman Brothers' Failure Matter?" *The New Yorker.com*, March 9, 2009; and Steve Stecklow and Diya Gullapalli, "A Money-Fund Manager's Fateful Shift," *Wall Street Journal*, December 8, 2008.

17. Michael E. Kerr and Murray Bowen, *Family Evaluation: The Role of the Family as an Emotional Unit that Governs Individual Behavior and Development* (New York: W.W. Norton & Company, 1988).

18. A. Bruce Steinwald, "Primary Care Professionals: Recent Supply Trends, Projections, and Valuation of Services," *Testimony Before the Committee on Health Education, Labor, and Pensions, U.S. Senate*, February 12, 2008.

19. Boris Groysberg, Ashish Nanda, and Nitin Nohria, "The Risky Business of Hiring Stars," *Harvard Business Review*, May 2004, 92–100; and Ulrike Malmendier and Geoffrey Tate, "Superstar CEOs," working paper no. 14140, NBER, June 2008.

20. Groysberg, Nanda, and Nohria, "The Risky Business of Hiring Stars"; and Boris Groysberg, Lex Sant, and Robin Abrams, "How to Minimize the Risks of Hiring Outside Stars," *Wall Street Journal*, September 22, 2008.

21. Geoffrey B. West and James H. Brown, "Life's Universal Scaling Laws," *Physics Today*, September 2004, 36–42.

22. Charles Perrow, *Normal Accidents: Living with High-Risk Technologies* (Princeton, NJ: Princeton University Press, 1999). See also Richard Bookstaber, *A Demon of Our Own Design: Markets, Hedge Funds, and the Perils of Financial Innovation* (New York: John Wiley & Sons, 2007); and Laurence Gonzales, *Deep Survival: Who Lives, Who Dies, and Why* (New York: W.W. Norton, 2003), 93–109.

23. John D. Sterman, *Business Dynamics: Systems Thinking and Modeling for a Complex World* (Boston: Irwin McGraw-Hill, 2000).

24. John D. Sterman, "Teaching Takes Off: Flight Simulations for Management Education," http://web.mit.edu/jsterman/www/SDG/beergame.html.

25. Jay W. Forrester, "Counterintuitive Behavior of Social Systems," *Testimony Before the Subcommittee on Urban Growth of the Committee on Banking and Currency, U.S. House of Representatives*, October 7, 1970.

26. Dhananjay K. Gode and Shyam Sunder, "Allocative Efficiency of Markets with Zero Intelligence Traders: Market as a Partial Substitute for Individual Rationality," *The Journal of Political Economy* 101, no. 1 (1993): 119–137.

Chapter 6— Evidence of Circumstance: How Outsourcing the Dreamliner
Became Boeing's Nightmare

1. Frank J. Sulloway, *Born to Rebel: Birth Order, Family Dynamics, and Creative Lives* (New York: Pantheon, 1996).

2. Rex Dalton, "Quarrel Over Book Leads to Call For Misconduct Inquiry," *Nature* 431 (October 21, 2004): 889; Judith Rich Harris, *The Nurture Assumption: Why Children Turn Out the Way They Do* (New York: Free Press, 1998), 365–378; Frederic Townsend, "Birth Order and Rebelliousness: Reconstructing the Research in *Born to Rebel*," *Politics and the Life Sciences* 19, no. 2 (2000): 135–156; Steven Pinker, *The Blank Slate: The Modern Denial of Human Nature* (New York: Viking, 2002),

389–390; and Judith Rich Harris, *No Two Alike: Human Nature and Human Individuality* (New York: W.W. Norton & Company, 2006), 83–114.

3. John Horgan, *The Undiscovered Mind: How the Human Brain Defies Replication, Medication, and Explanation* (New York: Free Press, 1999), 192.

4. Susan Goldsmith, "Frank's War," *East Bay Express*, April 28, 2004.

5. Philip Zimbardo, *The Lucifer Effect: Understanding How Good People Turn Evil* (New York: Random House, 2007); Cécile Ernst and Jules Angst, *Birth Order: Its Influence on Personality* (Berlin: Springer-Verlag, 1983), 284; and Jeremy Freese, Brian Powell, and Lala Carr Steelman, "Rebel Without a Cause or Effect: Birth Order and Social Attitudes," *American Sociological Review* 64, no. 2 (1999): 207–231.

6. Paul R. Carlile and Clayton M. Christensen, "The Cycles of Theory Building in Management Research," Harvard Business School Working Paper Series, no. 05–057, 2005; and Barney G. Glaser and Anselm L. Strauss, *The Discovery of Grounded Theory: Strategies for Qualitative Research* (New Brunswick, NJ: Aldine, 1967).

7. Dominic Gates, "Boeing May Junk Worldwide Assembly for Next Jet," *Seattle Times*, November 1, 2007; James Wallace, "Boeing Executive Faults Some 787 Suppliers," *Seattle Post-Intelligencer*, November 1, 2007; J. Lynn Lunsford, "Boeing Scramble to Repair Problems With New Plane," *Wall Street Journal*, December 7, 2007; and J. Lynn Lunsford, "Outsourcing at Crux of Boeing Strike," *Wall Street Journal*, September 8, 2008.

8. Clayton M. Christensen, Matt Verlinden, and George Westerman, "Disruption, Disintegration and the Dissipation of Differentiability," *Industrial and Corporate Change* 11, no. 5 (2002): 955–993; and Carliss Y. Baldwin and Kim B. Clark, *Design Rules: The Power of Modularity* (Cambridge: MIT Press, 2000).

9. For a formal treatment of the Colonel Blotto game, see Brian Roberson, "The Colonel Blotto Game," *Economic Theory* 29, no. 1 (2006): 1–24; for a more informal discussion, see Scott E. Page, *The Difference: How the Power of Diversity Creates Better Groups, Firms, Schools, and Societies* (Princeton, NJ: Princeton University Press, 2007), 112–114; and Jeffrey Kluger, *Simplexity: Why Simple Things Become Complex* (and *How Complex Things Can Be Made Simple*) (New York: Hyperion, 2008), 183–185.

10. Russell Golman and Scott E. Page, "General Blotto: Games of Allocative Strategic Mismatch," *Public Choice*, 138, no. 3 (2009): 279–299.

11. For this example, I selected an Xa/Xb ratio of 0.13. Using Theorem 3 from Roberson, "The Colonel Blotto Game," the expected payoff is 2.5 percent when n equals 9. Using Theorem 2, the expected payoff is 6.7 percent when n equals 15.

12. Eli Ben-Naim, Federico Vazquez, and Sidney Redner, "Parity and Predictability of Competitions," *Journal of Quantitative Analysis in Sports* 2, no. 4 (2006): 1–12.

13. Professor Jonathan Partington hosted a 100-point, 10-battlefied tournament in 1990. He found the strategies highly nontransitive. Of over 100 entries, Paul Taylor was the winner. His strategy was (17, 3, 17, 3, 17, 3, 17, 3, 17, 3). See http://www.amsta.leeds.ac.uk/~pmt6jrp/personal/blotto.html.

14. Based on Page, *The Difference*, 113.

15. David J. Leinweber, "Stupid Data Miner Tricks: Overfitting the S&P 500," *The Journal of Investing*, 16, no. 1 (2007): 15–22; and Phil Rosenzweig, *The Halo*

Effect . . . and the Eight Other Business Delusions That Deceive Managers (New York: Free Press, 2007), 72–75.

16. Judea Pearl, *Causality: Models, Reasoning, and Inference* (Cambridge: Cambridge University Press, 2000); Stephen L. Morgan and Christopher Winship, eds., *Counterfactuals and Causal Inference: Methods and Principles for Social Research* (Cambridge: Cambridge University Press, 2007); and Paul R. Rosenbaum, *Observational Studies,* 2nd ed. (New York: Springer, 2002).

17. David A. Kenny, *Correlation and Causality* (New York: John Wiley & Sons, 1979); and B. Shannon, J. Peacock, and M. J. Brown, "Body fatness, television viewing and calorie-intake of a sample of Pennsylvania sixth grade children," *Journal of Nutrition Education* 23, no. 6 (1991): 262–268.

18. Jared Diamond, *Collapse: How Societies Choose to Fail or Succeed* (New York: Viking, 2005), 211–276.

19. Clayton M. Christensen, *The Innovator's Dilemma: When New Technologies Cause Great Companies to Fail* (Boston: Harvard Business School Press, 1997); and author's personal correspondence with Thomas Thurston.

20. Eric D. Beinhocker, *The Origin of Wealth: Evolution, Complexity, and the Radical Remaking of Economics* (Boston: Harvard Business School Press, 2006); and Kathleen M. Eisenhardt and Donald N. Sull, "Strategy as Simple Rules," *Harvard Business Review*, January 2001, 107–116.

21. David Halberstam, *The Education of a Coach* (New York: Hyperion, 2005), 46–51.

Chapter 7 — Grand Ah-Whooms: How Ten Brits Made the Millennium Bridge Wobble

1. I initially learned about the Millennium Bridge from Steve Strogatz. See Steven Strogatz, *Sync: The Emerging Science of Spontaneous Order* (New York: Hyperion, 2003), 171–176. See also Nonie Niesewand, "Will Norman Foster and Anthony Caro Cross the Thames in a Blade of Light?" *The Independent*, September 25, 1997.

2. Pat Dallard, Tony Fitzpatrick, Anthony Flint, Angus Low, Roger Ridsdill Smith, Michael Willford, and Mark Roche, "London Millennium Bridge: Pedestrian-Induced Lateral Vibration," *Journal of Bridge Engineering* 6, no. 6 (2001): 412–417; and Deyan Sudjic, *Blade of Light: The Story of London's Millennium Bridge* (London: Penguin Books, 2001).

3. Andy Beckett, "Shaken Not Sturdy," *The Guardian*, July 18, 2000.

4. Philip Ball, *Critical Mass: How One Thing Leads to Another* (New York: Farrar, Straus and Giroux, 2004), 80–97. Ball takes the term "the grand ah-whoom" from Kurt Vonnegut's book, *Cat's Cradle*. See also Malcolm Gladwell, *The Tipping Point: How Little Things Can Make a Big Difference* (New York: Little, Brown and Company, 2000).

5. Per Bak, *How Nature Works: The Science of Self-Organized* Criticality (New York: Springer-Verlag, 1996); and John H. Holland, *Hidden Order: How Adaption Builds Complexity* (Reading, MA: Addison-Wesley, 1995), 39–40.

6. Steven H. Strogatz, Daniel M. Abrams, Allan McRobie, Bruno Eckhardt, and Edward Ott, "Crowd Synchrony on the Millennium Bridge," *Nature* 483 (November 3, 2005): 43–44.

7. Neal J. Roese and James M. Olsen, eds., *What Might Have Been: The Social Psychology of Counterfactual Thinking* (Mahwah, NJ: Lawrence Erlbaum Associates, 1994).

8. M. E. J. Newman, "Power Laws, Pareto Distributions and Zipf's Law," *arXiv:condmat*, May 29, 2006; Chris Anderson, *The Long Tail: Why the Future of Business is Selling Less of More* (New York: Hyperion, 2006); and Arthur DeVany, *Hollywood Economics: How Extreme Uncertainty Shapes the Film Industry* (New York: Routledge, 2004).

9. Nassim Nicholas Taleb, *The Black Swan: The Impact of the Highly Improbable* (New York: Random House, 2007), xvii–xviii.

10. James Surowiecki, *The Wisdom of Crowds: Why the Many Are Smarter Than the Few and How Collective Wisdom Shapes Business, Economies, Societies, and Nations* (New York: Doubleday and Company, 2004).

11. Blake LeBaron, "Financial Market Efficiency in a Coevolutionary Environment," *Proceedings of the Workshop on Simulation of Social Agents: Architectures and Institutions, Argonne National Laboratory and University of Chicago*, October 2000, Argonne 2001, 33–51; Paul Ehrlich and Brian Walker, "Rivets and Redundancy," *BioScience* 48, no. 5 (1998): 387; Robert M. May, *Complexity and Stability in Model Ecosystems* (Princeton, NJ: Princeton University Press, 1974); and Robert M. May, Simon A. Levin, and George Sugihara, "Ecology for Bankers," *Nature* 451 (February 21, 2008): 893–895.

12. Bertrand Russell, *The Problems of Philosophy* (Oxford: Oxford University Press, 1959); Taleb, *The Black Swan*, 40–41; and Hyman P. Minsky, *Stabilizing an Unstable Economy* (New Haven, CT: Yale University Press, 1986). For an example of how investors extrapolate, see Hersh Shefrin, *Behavioral Corporate Finance: Decisions That Create Value* (New York: McGraw Hill, 2007), 66–68.

13. Francesco Guerrera, "Merrill Losses Wipe Away Longtime Profits," *Financial Times*, August 28, 2008.

14. Karl Duncker, "On Problem Solving," *Psychological Monographs* 58, no. 270 (1945); Paul J. Feltovich, Rand J. Spiro, and Richard L. Coulsen, "Issues of Expert Flexibility in Contexts Characterized by Complexity and Change," in *Expertise in Context: Human and Machine*, ed. Paul J. Feltovich, Kenneth M. Ford, and Robert R. Hoffman (Menlo Park, CA, and Cambridge, MA: AAAI Press and MIT Press, 1997), 125–146. Taleb, *The Black Swan*, discusses a similar concept he calls the "ludic fallacy."

15. Donald MacKenzie, *An Engine, Not a Camera: How Financial Models Shape Markets* (Cambridge: MIT Press, 2006).

16. Benoit Mandelbrot, "The Variation of Certain Speculative Prices," in *The Random Character of Stock Market Prices*, ed. Paul H. Cootner, (Cambridge: MIT Press, 1964), 369–412. This is also a core theme of Taleb, *The Black Swan*. See also Benoit Mandelbrot and Richard L. Hudson, *The (Mis)Behavior of Markets* (New York: Basic Books, 2004).

17. Paul H. Cootner, "Comments on The Variation of Certain Speculative Prices," in Cootner, *The Random Character of Stock Market Prices*, 413–418.

18. Philip Mirowski, *The Effortless Economy of Science?* (Durham, NC: Duke University Press, 2004), 232.

19. Felix Salmon, "Recipe for Disaster: The Formula That Killed Wall Street," *Wired Magazine*, March 2009, 74–79, 112.; and MacKenzie, *An Engine, Not a Camera,* 223 and 233.

20. Stephen Jay Gould, *Wonderful Life: The Burgess Shale and the Nature of History* (New York: W.W. Norton & Company, 1989), 292–323.

21. Matthew J. Salganik, Peter Sheridan Dodds, and Duncan J. Watts, "Experimental Study of Inequality and Unpredictability in an Artificial Cultural Market," *Science* 311 (February 10, 2006): 854–856. For a treatment in the popular press, see Duncan J. Watts, "Is Justin Timberlake a Product of Cumulative Advantage?" *New York Times Magazine*, April 15, 2007.

22. Paul Pierson, *Politics in Time: History, Institutions, and Social Analysis* (Princeton, NJ: Princeton University Press, 2004); and W. Brian Arthur, *Increasing Returns and Path Dependence in the Economy* (Ann Arbor, MI: University of Michigan Press, 1994).

23. Scott E. Page, "Path Dependence," *Quarterly Journal of Political Science* 1, no. 1 (2006): 87–115.

24. Arthur, *Increasing Returns and Path Dependence in the Economy*; Gladwell, *The Tipping Point*; and Richard Brodie, *Virus of the Mind: The New Science of the Meme* (Seattle, WA: Integral Press, 1996).

25. For the stock market, see Didier Sornette, *Why Stock Markets Crash: Critical Events in Complex Financial Systems* (Princeton, NJ: Princeton University Press, 2003); for terrorist acts, see Aaron Clauset and Maxwell Young, "Scale Invariance in Global Terrorism," *arXiv:physics*, May 1, 2005; and for power grid, see Jie Chen, James S. Thorp, and Ian Dobson, "Cascading Dynamics and Mitigation Assessment in Power System Disturbances Via a Hidden Failure Model," *Electrical Power and Energy Systems* 27 (2005): 318–326.

26. Shankar Vedantam, "Vote Your Conscience. If You Can." *Washington Post*, December 31, 2007, A3.

27. Edward O. Thorp, *The Mathematics of Gambling* (Hollywood, CA: Gambling Times, 1984); J. L. Kelly Jr., "A New Interpretation of Information Rate," *Bell System Technical Journal*, 1956, 917–926; and William Poundstone, *Fortune's Formula: The Untold Story of the Unscientific Betting System that Beat The Casinos and Wall Street* (New York: Hill and Wang, 2005).

28. Michael Lewis, "The Natural-Catastrophe Casino," *New York Times Magazine*, August 26, 2007.

29. Jason Zweig, "Peter Bernstein Interview: He May Know More About Investing than Anyone Alive," *Money Magazine*, November, 2004, 143–148.

Chapter 8 — Sorting Luck from Skill: Why Investors Excel at Buying High and Selling Low

1. Tyler Kepner, "With Only 150 Games to Go, Steinbrenner Checks In," *New York Times*, April 18, 2005.

2. Stephen M. Stigler, *Statistics on the Table: The History of Statistical Concepts and Methods* (Cambridge: Harvard University Press, 1999), 173–188.

3. Michael Bulmer, *Francis Galton: Pioneer of Heredity and Biometry* (Baltimore, MD: John Hopkins University Press, 2003), 212–215.

4. Francis Galton, "Regression towards Mediocrity in Hereditary Stature," *Journal of the Anthropological Institute* 15 (1886): 252; Francis Galton, *Natural Inheritance* (London: MacMillan, 1889); and Peter L. Bernstein, *Against the Gods: The Remarkable Story of Risk* (New York: John Wiley & Sons, 1996), 152–171.

5. For an excellent account of Galton's work, see Stephen M. Stigler, *The History of Statistics: The Measurement of Uncertainty before 1990* (Cambridge: Harvard University Press, 1986), 265–299.

6. Stigler, *Statistics on the Table*.

7. See http://www.edge.org/images/Kahneman_large.jpg.

8. Amit Goyal and Sunil Wahal, "The Selection and Termination of Investment Management Firms by Plan Sponsors," *The Journal of Finance* 63, no. 4 (2008): 1805–1847.

9. Michael Mauboussin, "Where Fools Rush In," *Time*, November 4, 2006, A44.

10. Michael J. Mauboussin, "Common Errors in DCF Models," *Mauboussin on Strategy*, March 23, 2006.

11. Horace Secrist, *The Triumph of Mediocrity in Business* (Evanston, IL: Bureau of Business Research, Northwestern University, 1933). This discussion was informed by Stigler, *Statistics on the Table*.

12. In some cases, companies may enjoy increasing returns for a time. See W. Brian Arthur, "Increasing Returns and the New World of Business," *Harvard Business Review*, July–August 1996, 101–109; and Carl Shapiro and Hal Varian, *Information Rules: A Strategic Guide to the Network Economy* (Boston: Harvard Business School Press, 1998).

13. Harold Hotelling, "Reviewed work: *The Triumph of Mediocrity in Business* by Horace Secrist," *Journal of the American Statistical Association* 28, no. 184 (1933): 463–465.

14. Stephen M. Stigler, "Milton Friedman and Statistics," in *The Collected Writings of Milton Friedman*, ed. Robert Leeson (New York: Routledge, forthcoming).

15. Jason Zweig, "Do You Sabotage Yourself? Daniel Kahneman Has Done More Than Anyone Else to Explain Why Most of Us Make So Many Mistakes as Investors—And What We Can Do About It," *Money*, May 1, 2001, 74–78. See also Thomas Gilovich, *How We Know What Isn't So: The Fallibility of Human Reason in Everyday Life* (New York: Free Press, 1991), 27–28.

16. Edward L. Thorndike, "A Constant Error in Psychological Ratings," *Journal of Applied Psychology* 4, no.1 (1920): 469–477.

17. Phil Rosenzweig, *The Halo Effect . . . and the Eight Other Business Delusions That Deceive Managers* (New York: Free Press, 2007).

18. Phil Rosenzweig "The Halo Effect and Other Managerial Delusions," *The McKinsey Quarterly*, February 2007, 77–85.

19. Dan Bilefsky and Anita Raghavan, "Blown Fuse: How 'Europe's GE' and Its Star CEO Tumbled to Earth," *Wall Street Journal,* January 23, 2003.

20. Richard Tomlinson and Paola Hjelt, "Dethroning Percy Barnevik," *Fortune International*, April 1, 2002, 38–41.

21. Tom Arnold, John H. Earl Jr., and David S. North, "Are Cover Stories Effective Contrarian Indicators?" *Financial Analysts Journal* 63, no. 2 (2007): 70–75.

See also Alexander Wolff, "SI Flashback: That Old Black Magic," *Sports Illustrated*, January 21, 2002.

22. Ray Murphy and Rod Truesdell, eds., *Ron Shandler's Baseball Forecaster 2008* (Roanoke, VA: Shandler Enterprises, 2007), 10–12.

23. Annie Duke, "Testimony before the House Committee on the Judiciary," November 14, 2007.

24. Amos Tversky and Daniel Kahneman, "Belief in the Law of Small Numbers," *Psychological Bulletin* 76, no. 2 (1971): 105–110.

25. Michael Lewis, *Moneyball: The Art of Winning an Unfair Game* (New York: W.W. Norton & Company, 2003), 274. See also Nassim Nicholas Taleb, *Fooled by Randomness: The Hidden Role of Chance in Life and in the Markets,* 2nd ed. (New York: Thomson Texere, 2004), 64–68.

26. Michael Bar-Eli, Simcha Avugos, and Markus Raab, "Twenty Years of 'Hot Hand' Research: Review and Critique," *Psychology of Sport and Exercise* 7, no. 6 (2006): 525–553.

27. Jerker Denrell, "Why Most People Disapprove of Me: Experience Sampling in Impression Formation," *Psychological Review* 112, no. 4 (2005): 951–978.

28. Stephen Jay Gould, *Full House: The Spread of Excellence from Plato to Darwin* (New York: Harmony Books, 1996), 109.

Conclusion—Time to Think Twice: How You Can Change Your Decision Making Immediately

1. John Allen Paulos, *A Mathematician Reads the Newspaper* (New York: Basic Books, 1995).

2. Philip Maymin, "Music and the Market: Song and Stock Market Volatility," Working paper, SSRN, November 4, 2008.

3. Avinash K. Dixit and Barry J. Nalebuff, *The Art of Strategy: A Game Theorist's Guide to Success in Business and Life* (New York: W.W. Norton & Company, 2008).

4. Tadeusz Tyszka and Piotr Zielonka, "Expert Judgments: Financial Analysts Versus Weather Forecasters," *The Journal of Psychology and Financial Markets* 3, no. 3 (2002): 152–160.

5. Philip E. Tetlock, *Expert Political Judgment: How Good Is It? How Can We Know?* (Princeton, NJ: Princeton University Press, 2005), 129–143.

6. Josh Waitzkin, *The Art of Learning: A Journey in the Pursuit of Excellence* (New York: Free Press, 2007), 212–213.

7. Atul A. Gawande, MD, et al., "A Surgical Checklist to Reduce Morbidity and Mortality in a Global Population," *New England Journal of Medicine* 360, no. 5 (20009): 491–499. See also Peter Bevelin, *Seeking Wisdom: From Darwin to Munger,* 3rd ed. (Malmö, Sweden: Post Scriptum AB, 2007), 287–296.

8. Gary Klein, "Performing a Project *Premortem*," *Harvard Business Review*, September 2007, 18–19; and Deborah J. Mitchell, J. Edward Russo, and Nancy Pennington, "Back to the Future: Temporal Perspective in the Explanation of Events," *Journal of Behavioral Decision Making* 2, no. 1 (1989): 25–38.

9. Warren E. Buffett, "Chairman's Letter," *Berkshire Hathaway Annual Report to Shareholders*, 1996.

Abernathy, Charles M., and Robert M. Hamm. *Surgical Intuition: What It Is and How to Get It*. Philadelphia, PA: Hanley & Belfus, 1995.

Akerlof, George A., and Robert J. Shiller. *Animal Spirits: How Human Psychology Drives the Economy, and Why It Matters For Global Capitalism*. Princeton, NJ: Princeton University Press, 2009.

Alicke, Mark D., and Olesya Govorun. "The Better-Than-Average Effect." In *The Self in Social Judgment*, edited by Mark D. Alicke, David A. Dunning, and Joachim I. Krueger, 85–106. New York: Psychology Press, 2005.

Anderson, Camilla. "Iceland Gets Help to Recover from Historic Crisis." *IMF Survey Online*, December 2, 2008.

Anderson, Chris. *The Long Tail: Why the Future of Business Is Selling Less of More*. New York: Hyperion, 2006.

Anderson, P. W. "More is Different." *Science* 177, no. 4047 (1972): 393–396.

Ariely, Dan. *Predictably Irrational: The Hidden Forces That Shape Our Decisions*. New York: Harper, 2008.

Armstrong, J. Scott. "Combining Forecasts." In *Principles of Forecasting: A Handbook for Researchers and Practitioners*, edited by J. Scott Armstrong, 417–439. New York: Springer, 2001.

Armstrong, J. Scott, Monica Adya, and Fred Collopy. "Rule-Based Forecasting: Using Judgment in Time-Series Extrapolation." In *Principles of Forecasting: A Handbook for Researchers and Practitioners*, edited by J. Scott Armstrong, 259–282. New York: Springer, 2001.

Arnold, Tom, John H. Earl Jr., and David S. North. "Are Cover Stories Effective Contrarian Indicators?" *Financial Analysts Journal* 63, no. 2 (2007): 70–75.

Arrow, Kenneth J., Robert Forsythe, Michael Gorham, Robert Hahn, Robin Hansen, John O. Ledyard, Saul Levmore, Robert Litan, Paul Milgrom, Forrest D. Nelson, George R. Neumann, Marco Ottaviani, Thomas C. Schelling, Robert J. Shiller, Vernon L. Smith, Erik Snowberg, Cass R. Sunstein, Paul C. Tetlock, Philip E. Tetlock, Hal R. Varian, Justin Wolfers, and Eric Zitzewitz. "The Promise of Prediction Markets." *Science* 320 (May 16, 2008): 877–878.

Arthur, W. Brian. *Increasing Returns and Path Dependence in the Economy*. Ann Arbor, MI: University of Michigan Press, 1994.

_____."Increasing Returns and the New World of Business." *Harvard Business Review*, July–August 1996, 101–109.

Asch, S. E. "Effects of Group Pressure Upon the Modification and Distortion of Judgments." In *Groups, Leadership and Men*, edited by Harold Guetzkow, 177–190. Pittsburgh, PA: Carnegie Press, 1951.

Ashenfelter, Orley. "Predicting the Quality and Prices of Bordeaux Wines." Working paper no. 4, American Association of Wine Economists, April 2007.

Ashton, John F. *In Six Days: Why Fifty Scientists Choose to Believe in Creation.* Green Forest, AR: Master Books, 2001.

Ayres, Ian. *Super Crunchers: Why Thinking-by-Numbers Is the New Way to be Smart.* New York: Bantam Books, 2007.

Bak, Per. *How Nature Works: The Science of Self-Organized Criticality.* New York: Springer-Verlag, 1996.

Baldwin, Carliss Y., and Kim B. Clark. *Design Rules: The Power of Modularity.* Cambridge: MIT Press, 2000.

Ball, Philip. *Critical Mass: How One Thing Leads to Another.* New York: Farrar, Straus and Giroux, 2004.

Bar-Eli, Michael, Simcha Avugos, Markus Raab. "Twenty Years of 'Hot Hand' Research: Review and Critique." *Psychology of Sport and Exercise* 7, no. 6 (2006): 525–553.

Bargh, John A., Mark Chen, and Laura Burrows. "Automaticity of Social Behavior: Direct Effects of Trait Construction and Stereotype Activation on Action," *Journal of Personality and Social Psychology* 71, no. 2 (1996): 230–244.

Barras, Laurent, O. Scaillet, and Russ R. Wermers. "False Discoveries in Mutual Fund Performance: Measuring Luck in Estimated Alphas," Robert H. Smith School Research paper RH 06-043, Swiss Finance Institute Research paper 08-18, September 1, 2008.

Bazerman, Max H. *Judgment in Managerial Decision Making.* 6th ed. New York: John Wiley & Sons, 2006.

Bazerman, Max H., and Michael D. Watkins. *Predictable Surprises: The Disasters You Should Have Seen Coming and How to Prevent Them.* Boston: Harvard Business School Press, 2004.

Bazerman, Max H., George Loewenstein, and Don A. Moore. "Why Good Accountants Do Bad Audits." *Harvard Business Review,* November 2002, 97–102.

Beckett, Andy. "Shaken Not Sturdy." *The Guardian,* July 18, 2000.

Beinhocker, Eric D. *The Origin of Wealth: Evolution, Complexity, and the Radical Remaking of Economics.* Boston: Harvard Business School Press, 2006.

Belongia, Michael T. "Predicting Interest Rates: A Comparison of Professional and Market-Based Forecasts." *Federal Reserve Bank of St. Louis,* March 1987, 9–15.

Ben-Naim, Eli, Federico Vazquez, and Sidney Redner. "Parity and Predictability of Competitions." *Journal of Quantitative Analysis in Sports* 2, no. 4 (2006): 1–12.

Berreby, David. *Us and Them: Understanding Your Tribal Mind.* New York: Little, Brown and Company, 2005.

Berns, Gregory. *Iconoclast: A Neuroscientist Reveals How to Think Differently.* Boston: Harvard Business Press, 2008.

Berns, Gregory S., Jonathan Chappelow, Caroline F. Zink, Giuseppe Pagnoni, Megan Martin-Skurski, and Jim Richards. "Neurobiological Correlates of Social Conformity and Independence During Mental Rotation," *Biological Psychiatry* 5, no. 8 (2005): 245–253.

Bernstein, Peter L. *Against the Gods: The Remarkable Story of Risk.* New York: John Wiley & Sons, 1996.

Bevelin, Peter. *Seeking Wisdom: From Darwin to Munger.* 3rd ed. Malmö, Sweden: Post Scriptum AB, 2007.

Blakeslee, Sandra. "What Other People Say May Change What You See." *New York Times,* June 28, 2005.

Bloch, Arthur. *Murphy's Law: The 26th Anniversary Edition*. New York: Perigee Trade, 2003.

Bonabeau, Eric. "Don't Trust Your Gut." *Harvard Business Review*, May 2003, 116–123.

Bonabeau, Eric, Marco Dorigo, and Guy Théraulaz. *Swarm Intelligence: From Natural to Artificial Systems*. New York: Oxford University Press, 1999.

Bonabeau, Eric, and Guy Théraulaz. "Swarm Smarts." *Scientific American*, March 2000, 82–90.

Bookstaber, Richard. *A Demon of Our Own Design: Markets, Hedge Funds, and the Perils of Financial Innovation*. New York: John Wiley & Sons, 2007.

Bower, Chuck, and Frank Frigo. "What Was Coach Thinking?" *New York Times*, February 1, 2009.

Brodie, Richard. *Virus of the Mind: The New Science of the Meme*. Seattle, WA: Integral Press, 1996.

Buchanan, Bruce G., Randall Davis, and Edward A. Feigenbaum. "Expert Systems: A Perspective from Computer Science." In *The Cambridge Handbook of Expertise and Expert Performance*, edited by K. Anders Ericsson, Neil Charness, Paul J. Feltovich, and Robert R. Hoffman, 87–103. Cambridge: Cambridge University Press, 2006.

Buehler, Roger, Dale Griffin, and Michael Ross. "Inside the Planning Fallacy: The Causes and Consequences of Optimistic Time Predictions." In *Heuristics and Biases: The Psychology of Intuitive Judgment*, edited by Thomas Gilovich, Dale Griffin, and Daniel Kahneman, 250–270. Cambridge: Cambridge University Press, 2002.

Buffett, Warren E. "Chairman's Letter." *Berkshire Hathaway Annual Report to Shareholders*, 1989.

_____. "Chairman's Letter." *Berkshire Hathaway Annual Report to Shareholders*, 1996.

Bulmer, Michael. *Francis Galton: Pioneer of Heredity and Biometry*. Baltimore, MD: The John Hopkins University Press, 2003.

Burger, Jerry M. "Replicating Milgram: Would People Still Obey Today?" *American Psychologist* 64, no. 1 (2009): 1–11.

Camerer, Colin F., Teck-Hua Ho, and Juin-Kuan Chong. "A Cognitive Hierarchy Model of Games." *The Quarterly Journal of Economics* 119, no. 3 (2004): 861–898.

Carlile, Paul R., and Clayton M. Christensen. "The Cycles of Theory Building in Management Research." Harvard Business School Working Paper Series, no. 05–057, 2005.

Chase, Alston. *Playing God in Yellowstone: The Destruction of America's First National Park*. Boston: The Atlantic Monthly Press, 1986.

Chen, Jie, James S. Thorp, and Ian Dobson. "Cascading Dynamics and Mitigation Assessment in Power System Disturbances Via a Hidden Failure Model." *Electrical Power and Energy Systems* 27 (2005): 318–326.

Chi, Michelene T. H., Robert Glaser, and Marshall Farr, eds. *The Nature of Expertise*. Hillsdale, NJ: Lawrence Erlbaum Associates, 1988.

Christensen, Clayton M. *The Innovator's Dilemma: When New Technologies Cause Great Companies to Fail*. Boston: Harvard Business School Press, 1997.

Christensen, Clayton M., Matt Verlinden, and George Westerman. "Disruption, Disintegration and the Dissipation of Differentiability." *Industrial and Corporate Change* 11, no. 5 (2002): 955–993.

Chun, Marvin M., and René Marois. "The Dark Side of Visual Attention." *Current Opinion in Neurobiology* 12, no. 2 (2002): 184–189.

Cialdini, Robert B. *Influence: The Psychology of Persuasion.* Rev. ed. New York: Quill, 1993.

Clauset, Aaron, and Maxwell Young. "Scale Invariance in Global Terrorism." *arXiv physics*, May 1, 2005.

Collins, Jim. *Good to Great: Why Some Companies Make the Leap ... and Others Don't.* New York: Harper Business, 2001.

Colvin, Geoff. *Talent is Overrated: What Really Separates World-Class Performers from Everybody Else.* New York: Portfolio, 2008.

Cootner, Paul H., ed. *The Random Character of Stock Market Prices.* Cambridge: MIT Press, 1964.

Cootner, Paul H. "Comments on The Variation of Certain Speculative Prices." In *The Random Character of Stock Market Prices*, edited by Paul H. Cootner, 413–418. Cambridge: MIT Press, 1964.

Copeland, Tom, Tim Koller, and Jack Murrin. *Valuation: Measuring and Managing the Value of Companies*, 3rd ed. New York: John Wiley & Sons, 2000.

Cowgill, Bo, Justin Wolfers, and Eric Zitzewitz. "Using Prediction Markets to Track Information Flows: Evidence from Google." Working paper, 2008.

Cutler, David M., James M. Poterba, and Lawrence H. Summers. "What Moves Stock Prices?" *The Journal of Portfolio Management*, 15, no. 3 (Spring 1989): 4–12.

Dallard, Pat, Tony Fitzpatrick, Anthony Flint, Angus Low, Roger Ridsdill Smith, Michael Willford, and Mark Roche. "London Millennium Bridge: Pedestrian-Induced Lateral Vibration." *Journal of Bridge Engineering* 6, no. 6 (2001): 412–417.

Dalton, Rex. "Quarrel Over Book Leads to Call For Misconduct Inquiry." *Nature* 431 (October 21, 2004): 889.

Damasio, Antonio. *The Feeling of What Happens: Body and Emotion in the Making of Consciousness.* New York: Harcourt Brace & Company, 1999.

Dawes, Robyn M., David Faust, and Paul E. Meehl. "Clinical versus Actuarial Judgment." In *Heuristics and Biases: The Psychology of Intuitive Judgment*, edited by Thomas Gilovich, Dale Griffin, and Daniel Kahneman, 716–729. Cambridge: Cambridge University Press, 2002.

Dawkins, Richard. *The God Delusion.* Boston: Houghton Mifflin Company, 2006.

Deber, Raisa B. "Physicians in Health Care Management: The Patient-Physician Partnership: Decision Making, Problem Solving and the Desire to Participate." *Canadian Medical Association* 151, no. 4 (1994): 423–427.

Denrell, Jerker. "Why Most People Disapprove of Me: Experience Sampling in Impression Formation." *Psychological Review* 112, no. 4 (2005): 951–978.

DeVany, Arthur. *Hollywood Economics: How Extreme Uncertainty Shapes the Film Industry.* New York: Routledge, 2004.

Diamond, Jared. *Collapse: How Societies Choose to Fail or Succeed.* New York: Viking, 2005.

Dixit, Avinash K., and Barry J. Nalebuff. *The Art of Strategy: A Game Theorist's Guide to Success in Business and Life* New York: W.W. Norton & Company, 2008.

Drucker, Peter F. *Management Challenges for the 21st Century.* New York: HarperBusiness, 1999.

Duke, Annie. *Testimony before the House Committee on the Judiciary.* November 14, 2007.

Duncker, Karl. "On Problem Solving." *Psychological Monographs* 58, no. 270 (1945).

Dvorak, Phred. "Best Buy Taps 'Prediction Market.'" *Wall Street Journal,* September 16, 2008.

Dye, Renée. "The Promise of Prediction Markets: A Roundtable." *The McKinsey Quarterly,* no. 2 (2008): 83–93.

Eguiluz, Victor M., and Martin G. Zimmerman. "Transmission of Information and Herd Behavior: An Application to Financial Markets." *Physical Review Letters* 85, no. 26 (2000): 5659–5662.

Ehrlich, Paul, and Brian Walker. "Rivets and Redundancy." *BioScience* 48, no. 5 (1998): 387.

Eisenhardt, Kathleen M., and Donald N. Sull. "Strategy as Simple Rules." *Harvard Business Review,* January 2001, 107–116.

Ellenberg, Jordan. "The Netflix Challenge: This Psychologist Might Outsmart the Math Brains Competing for the Netflix Prize." *Wired Magazine,* March, 2008, 114–122.

Epley, Nicholas, and Thomas Gilovich. "The Anchoring-and-Adjustment Heuristic: Why the Adjustments Are Insufficient." *Psychological Science* 17, no. 4 (2006): 311–318.

Ernst, Cécile, and Jules Angst. *Birth Order: Its Influence on Personality.* Berlin: Springer-Verlag, 1983.

Fauconnier, Gilles, and Mark Turner. *The Way We Think: Conceptual Blending and the Mind's Hidden Complexities.* New York: Basic Books, 2002.

Feltovich, Paul J., Rand J. Spiro, and Richard L. Coulsen. "Issues of Expert Flexibility in Contexts Characterized by Complexity and Change." In *Expertise in Context: Human and Machine,* edited by Paul J. Feltovich, Kenneth M. Ford, and Robert R. Hoffman, Menlo Park, CA, and Cambridge. AAAI Press and MIT Press, 1997.

Festinger, Leon, Henry W. Riecken, and Stanley Schachter. *When Prophecy Fails: A Social and Psychological Study of a Modern Group that Predicted the Destruction of the World.* Minneapolis: University of Minnesota Press, 1956.

Forrester, Jay W. "Counterintuitive Behavior of Social Systems." *Testimony Before the Subcommittee on Urban Growth of the Committee on Banking and Currency, U.S. House of Representatives,* October 7, 1970.

Freese, Jeremy, Brian Powell, and Lala Carr Steelman. "Rebel Without a Cause or Effect: Birth Order and Social Attitudes." *American Sociological Review* 64, no. 2 (1999): 207–231.

French, Kenneth R. "Presidential Address: The Cost of Active Investing." *The Journal of Finance* 63, no. 4 (2008): 1537–1573.

Freymuth, Angela K., and George F. Ronan. "Modeling Patient Decision-Making: The Role of Base-Rate and Anecdotal Information." *Journal of Clinical Psychology in Medical Settings* 11, no. 3 (2004): 211–216.

Galinsky, Adam D., and Thomas Mussweiler. "First Offers as Anchors: The Role of Perspective-Taking and Negotiator Focus." *Journal of Personality and Social Psychology* 81, no. 4 (2001): 657–669.

Galton, Francis. "Regression towards Mediocrity in Hereditary Stature." *Journal of the Anthropological Institute* 15 (1886).

———. *Natural Inheritance.* London: MacMillan, 1889.

Gates, Dominic. "Boeing May Junk Worldwide Assembly for Next Jet." *Seattle Times*, November 1, 2007.

Gawande, Atul. "The Checklist." *The New Yorker*, December 10, 2007, 86–95.

———. "A Lifesaving Checklist." *New York Times*, December 30, 2007.

Gawande, Atul A. MD, et al. "A Surgical Checklist to Reduce Morbidity and Mortality in a Global Population." *New England Journal of Medicine* 360, no. 5 (2009): 491–499.

Gell-Mann, Murray. *The Quark and the Jaguar: Adventures in the Simple and the Complex.* New York: W.H. Freeman, 1994.

Gigerenzer, Gerd. *Gut Feelings: The Intelligence of the Unconscious.* New York: Viking, 2007.

Gilbert, Daniel. *Stumbling on Happiness.* New York: Alfred A. Knopf, 2006.

Gilovich, Thomas. *How We Know What Isn't So: The Fallibility of Human Reason in Everyday Life.* New York: Free Press, 1991.

Gilovich, Thomas, Dacher Keltner, and Richard E. Nisbett. *Social Psychology.* New York: W.W. Norton & Company, 2006.

Ginsberg, Matthew L. "Computers, Games and the Real World." *Scientific American Presents: Exploring Intelligence* 9, no. 4 (1998), 84–89.

Gladwell, Malcolm. *The Tipping Point: How Little Things Can Make a Big Difference.* New York: Little, Brown and Company, 2000.

———. *Blink: The Power of Thinking Without Thinking.* New York: Little, Brown and Company, 2005.

———. "Most Likely to Succeed: How Do We Hire When We Can't Tell Who's Right for the Job?" *The New Yorker*, December 15, 2008, 36–42.

Glaser, Barney G., and Anselm L. Strauss. *The Discovery of Grounded Theory: Strategies for Qualitative Research.* New Brunswick, NJ: Aldine, 1967.

Gode, Dhananjay K., and Shyam Sunder. "Allocative Efficiency of Markets with Zero Intelligence Traders: Market as a Partial Substitute for Individual Rationality." *The Journal of Political Economy* 101, no. 1 (1993): 119–137.

Golman, Russell, and Scott E. Page, "General Blotto: Games of Allocative Strategic Mismatch," *Public Choice*, 138, no. 3 (2009): 279–299.

Goldsmith, Susan. "Frank's War." *East Bay Express*, April 28, 2004.

Goldstein, Daniel G., Eric J. Johnson, Andreas Herrmann, and Mark Heitmann. "Nudge Your Customers Toward Better Choices." *Harvard Business Review*, December 2008, 99–105.

Gonzales, Laurence. *Deep Survival: Who Lives, Who Dies, and Why.* New York: W.W. Norton & Company, 2003.

———. *Everyday Survival: Why Smart People Do Stupid Things.* New York: W.W. Norton & Company, 2008.

Goodman, Billy. "Thinking about Thinking." *Princeton Alumni Weekly*, January 29, 2003, 26–27.

Goodwin, Doris Kearns. *Team of Rivals: The Political Genius of Abraham Lincoln.* New York: Simon & Schuster, 2005.

Gould, Stephen Jay. *Wonderful Life: The Burgess Shale and the Nature of History.* New York: W.W. Norton & Company, 1989.

_____. *Full House: The Spread of Excellence from Plato to Darwin.* New York: Harmony Books, 1996.

Goyal, Amit, and Sunil Wahal. "The Selection and Termination of Investment Management Firms by Plan Sponsors." *The Journal of Finance* 63, no. 4 (2008): 1805–1847.

Graham, John R., Campbell R. Harvey, and Shiva Rajgopal. "Value Destruction and Financial Reporting Decisions." *Financial Analysts Journal* 62, no. 6 (2006): 27–39.

Greenspan, Alan. *Testimony to the Committee of Government Oversight and Reform,* October 23, 2008.

Greenspan, Stephen. "Why We Keep Falling for Financial Scams." *Wall Street Journal,* January 3, 2009.

_____. *Annals of Gullibility: Why We Get Duped and How to Avoid It.* Westport, CT: Praeger, 2009.

Groopman, Jerome. *How Doctors Think.* Boston: Houghton Mifflin Company, 2007.

Grove, William M., David H. Zald, Boyd S. Lebow, Beth E. Snitz, and Chad Nelson. "Clinical Versus Mechanical Prediction: A Meta-Analysis." *Psychological Assessment* 12, no. 1 (2000): 19–30.

Groysberg, Boris, Ashish Nanda, and Nitin Nohria. "The Risky Business of Hiring Stars." *Harvard Business Review,* May 2004: 92–100.

Groysberg, Boris, Lex Sant, and Robin Abrams. "How to Minimize the Risks of Hiring Outside Stars." *Wall Street Journal,* September 22, 2008.

Guerrera, Francesco. "Merrill Losses Wipe Away Longtime Profits." *Financial Times,* August 28, 2008.

Guerrera, Francesco, and Julie MacIntosh. "Luck Played Part in Rohm and Haas Deal." *The Financial Times,* July 10, 2008.

Halberstam, David. *The Education of a Coach.* New York: Hyperion, 2005.

Hamel, Gary, with Bill Breen *The Future of Management.* Boston: Harvard Business School Press, 2007.

Hansell, Saul. "Google Answer to Filling Jobs Is an Algorithm." *New York Times,* January 3, 2007.

Harris, Judith Rich. *The Nurture Assumption: Why Children Turn Out the Way They Do.* New York: Free Press, 1998.

_____. *No Two Alike: Human Nature and Human Individuality.* New York: W.W. Norton & Company, 2006.

Hastie, Reid, and Robyn M. Dawes. *Rational Choice in an Uncertain World.* Thousand Oaks, CA: Sage Publications, 2001.

Hogarth, Robin M. *Educating Intuition.* Chicago: The University of Chicago Press, 2001.

Holland, John H. *Hidden Order: How Adaption Builds Complexity.* Reading, MA: Addison-Wesley, 1995.

Holland, Rob W., Merel Hendriks, and Henk Aarts. "Smells Like Clean Spirit: Nonconscious Effects of Scent on Cognition and Behavior." *Psychological Science* 16, no. 9 (2005): 689–693.

Horgan, John. *The Undiscovered Mind: How the Human Brain Defies Replication, Medication, and Explanation*. New York: Free Press, 1999.

Hotelling, Harold. "Reviewed work: *The Triumph of Mediocrity in Business* by Horace Secrist." *Journal of the American Statistical Association* 28, no. 184 (1933): 463–465.

Huettel, Scott A., Peter B. Mack, and Gregory McCarthy. "Perceiving Patterns in Random Series: Dynamic Processing of Sequence in Prefrontal Cortex." *Nature Neuroscience* 5, no. 5 (2002): 485–490.

James, William. *The Principles of Psychology*, vol. 1. New York: Henry Holt & Co., 1890.

Janis, Irving. *Groupthink: Psychological Studies of Policy Decisions and Fiascoes*. 2nd ed. Boston: Houghton Mifflin, 1982.

Jensen, Michael C. "The Performance of Mutual Funds in the Period 1945–1964." *The Journal of Finance* 23, no. 2 (1968): 389–416.

Johnson, Eric J., and Daniel Goldstein. "Do Defaults Save Lives?" *Science* 302 (November 21, 2003): 1338–1339.

Johnson, Steven. *Emergence: The Connected Lives of Ants, Brains, Cities, and Software*. New York: Scribner, 2001.

Johnson-Laird, Philip N. *Mental Models*. Cambridge: Harvard University Press, 1983.

_____. "Mental Models and Reasoning." In *The Nature of Reasoning*, edited by Jacqueline P. Leighton, and Robert J. Sternberg, 169–204. Cambridge: Cambridge University Press, 2004.

_____. *How We Reason*. Oxford: Oxford University Press, 2006.

Kahneman, Daniel. "Maps of Bounded Rationality: A Perspective on Intuitive Judgment and Choice." *Nobel Prize Lecture*, December 8, 2002.

Kahneman, Daniel, and Amos Tversky. "Prospect Theory: An Analysis of Decision Making Under Risk." *Econometrica* 47, no. 2 (1979): 263–291.

Kahneman, Daniel, and Amos Tversky. "Intuitive Prediction: Biases and Corrective Procedures." In *Judgment Under Uncertainty: Heuristics and Biases*, edited by Daniel Kahneman, Paul Slovic, and Amos Tversky, 414–421. Cambridge: Cambridge University Press, 1982.

Kahneman, Danny. "A Short Course in Thinking about Thinking." *Edge.org*, 2007.

Katz, Elihu, and Paul F. Lazarsfeld. *Personal Influence: The Part Played by People in the Flow of Mass Communications*. New York: Free Press, 1955.

Kaufman, Peter D., ed. *Poor Charlie's Almanack*. Expanded 2nd ed. Virginia Beach, VA: PCA Publication, 2006.

Kelly, J. L., Jr. "A New Interpretation of Information Rate." *Bell System Technical Journal* (1956): 917–926.

Kenny, David A. *Correlation and Causality*. New York: John Wiley & Sons, 1979.

Kepner, Tyler. "With Only 150 Games to Go, Steinbrenner Checks In." *New York Times*, April 18, 2005.

Kerr, Michael E., and Murray Bowen. *Family Evaluation: The Role of the Family as an Emotional Unit that Governs Individual Behavior and Development*. New York: W.W. Norton & Company, 1988.

Kierkegaard, Søren. *The Diary of Søren Kierkegaard*. New York: Carol Publishing Group, 1993.

Klein, Gary. *Sources of Power: How People Make Decisions*. Cambridge: MIT Press, 1998.

_____. "Performing a Project *Premortem*." *Harvard Business Review*, September 2007, 18–19.

Klingberg, Torkel. *The Overflowing Brain: Information Overload and the Limits of Working Knowledge*. New York: Oxford University Press, 2009.

Klinger, David. *Into the Kill Zone: A Cop's Eye View of Deadly Force*. San Francisco: Jossey-Bass, 2004.

Kluger, Jeffrey. *Simplexity: Why Simple Things Become Complex (and How Complex Things Can Be Made Simple)*. New York: Hyperion, 2008.

Kruger, Justin, and David Dunning. "Unskilled and Unaware of It: How Difficulties in Recognizing One's Own Incompetence Lead to Inflated Self-Assessments." *Journal of Personality and Social Psychology* 77, no. 6 (1999): 1121–1134.

Kuzmits, Frank E., and Arthur J. Adams. "The NFL Combine: Does It Predict Performance in the National Football League?" *The Journal of Strength and Conditioning Research* 22, no. 6 (2008): 1721–1727.

Langer, Ellen J. "The Illusion of Control." *Journal of Personality and Social Psychology* 32, no. 2 (1975): 311–328.

LeBaron, Blake. "Financial Market Efficiency in a Coevolutionary Environment." *Proceedings of the Workshop on Simulation of Social Agents: Architectures and Institutions, Argonne National Laboratory and University of Chicago, October 2000*, Argonne 2001, 33–51.

LeDoux, Joseph. *The Emotional Brain: The Mysterious Underpinnings of Emotional Life*. New York: Touchstone, 1996.

Leinweber, David J. "Stupid Data Miner Tricks: Overfitting the S&P 500." *Journal of Investing*, 16, no. 1 (2007): 15–22.

Leonhardt, David. "Why Doctors So Often Get It Wrong." *New York Times*, February 22, 2006.

Lewis, Michael. *Moneyball: The Art of Winning an Unfair Game*. New York: W.W. Norton & Company, 2003.

_____. "The Natural-Catastrophe Casino." *New York Times Magazine*, August 26, 2007.

_____. "Wall Street on the Tundra." *Vanity Fair*, April 2009, 140–147, 173–177.

Loewenstein, George F., Elke U. Weber, Christopher K. Hsee, and Ned Welch. "Risk as Feelings." *Psychological Bulletin* 127, no. 2 (2001): 267–286.

Lohr, Steve. "Betting to Improve the Odds." *New York Times*, April 9, 2008.

Lovallo, Dan, and Daniel Kahneman. "Delusions of Success." *Harvard Business Review*, July 2003, 56–63.

Loveman, Gary. "Diamonds in the Data Mine." *Harvard Business Review*, May 2003, 109–113.

Lowenstein, Roger. *When Genius Failed: The Rise and Fall of Long-Term Capital Management*. New York: Random House, 2000.

Lunsford, J. Lynn. "Boeing Scrambles to Repair Problems with New Plane." *Wall Street Journal*, December 7, 2007.

_____. "Outsourcing at Crux of Boeing Strike." *Wall Street Journal*, September 8, 2008.

MacGregor, Donald G. "Imagery and Financial Judgment." *The Journal of Psychology and Financial Markets* 3, no. 1 (2002): 15–22.

Mack, Arien, and Irvin Rock. *Inattentional Blindness*. Cambridge: MIT Press, 1998.

MacKenzie, Donald. *An Engine, Not a Camera: How Financial Models Shape Markets*. Cambridge: MIT Press, 2006.

Malhotra, Deepak, and Max H. Bazerman. *Negotiation Genius: How to Overcome Obstacles and Achieve Brilliant Results at the Bargaining Table and Beyond*. New York: Bantam Books, 2007.

Malkiel, Burton G. "Returns from Investing in Equity Mutual Funds 1971–1991." *The Journal of Finance* 50, no. 2 (1995): 549–572.

Malmendier, Ulrike, and Geoffrey Tate. "Superstar CEOs." Working paper 14140, NBER, June 2008.

Mandel, Naomi, and Eric J. Johnson. "When Web Pages Influence Choice: Effects of Visual Primes on Experts and Novices." *Journal of Consumer Research* 29, no. 2 (2002): 235–245.

Mandelbrot, Benoit. "The Variation of Certain Speculative Prices." In *The Random Character of Stock Market Prices*, edited by Paul H. Cootner, 369–412. Cambridge: MIT Press, 1964.

Mandelbrot, Benoit, and Richard L. Hudson. *The (Mis)Behavior of Markets*. New York: Basic Books, 2004.

March, James G. *A Primer on Decision Making: How Decisions Happen*. New York: Free Press, 1994.

Mauboussin, Michael. "Where Fools Rush In." *Time*, November 4, 2006, A44.

Mauboussin, Michael J. "Common Errors in DCF Models." *Mauboussin on Strategy*, March 23, 2006.

_____. "Explaining the Wisdom of Crowds: Applying the Logic of Diversity." *Mauboussin on Strategy*, March 20, 2007.

_____. "What Good Are Experts?" *Harvard Business Review*, February 2008, 43–44.

May, Robert M. *Complexity and Stability in Model Ecosystems*. Princeton, NJ: Princeton University Press, 1974.

May, Robert M., Simon A. Levin, and George Sugihara. "Ecology for Bankers." *Nature* 451 (February 21, 2008): 893–895.

Maymin, Philip. "Music and the Market: Song and Stock Market Volatility." Working paper, SSRN, November 4, 2008.

McCloskey, Deirdre N. *If You're So Smart: The Narrative of Economic Expertise*. Chicago: University of Chicago Press, 1990.

McClure, Samuel M., David I Laibson, George Loewsenstein, and Jonathan D. Cohen. "Separate Neural Systems Value Immediate and Delayed Monetary Rewards." *Science* 306 (October 15, 2004): 503–507.

Meehl, Paul E. *Clinical versus Statistical Prediction: A Theoretical Analysis and a Review of the Evidence*. Minneapolis: University of Minnesota Press, 1954.

Merton, Robert K. "The Unanticipated Consequences of Purposive Social Action." *American Sociological Review* 1, no. 6 (1936): 894–904.

Milgram, Stanley. *Obedience to Authority*. New York: Harper & Row, 1974.

Miller, John H., and Scott E. Page. *Complex Adaptive Systems: An Introduction to Computational Models of Social Life.* Princeton, NJ: Princeton University Press, 2007.

Miller, Peter. "The Genius of Swarms." *National Geographic,* July 2007, 126–147.

Minsky, Hyman P. *Stabilizing an Unstable Economy.* New Haven, CT: Yale University Press, 1986.

Mirowski, Philip. *The Effortless Economy of Science?* Durham, NC: Duke University Press, 2004.

Mitchell, Deborah J., J. Edward Russo, and Nancy Pennington. "Back to the Future: Temporal Perspective in the Explanation of Events." *Journal of Behavioral Decision Making* 2, No. 1 (1989): 25–38.

Moore, Don A., Philip E. Tetlock, Lloyd Tanlu, and Max H. Bazerman. "Conflicts of Interest and the Case of Auditor Independence: Moral Seduction and Strategic Issue Cycling." *Academy of Management Review* 31, no. 1 (2006): 10–29.

Morgan, Stephen L., and Christopher Winship, eds. *Counterfactuals and Causal Inference: Methods and Principles for Social Research.* Cambridge: Cambridge University Press, 2007.

Morris, Michael W., and Kaiping Peng. "Culture and Cause: American and Chinese Attributions for Social and Physical Events." *Journal of Personality and Social Psychology* 67, no. 6 (1994): 949–971.

Murphy, Ray, and Rod Truesdell, eds. *Ron Shandler's Baseball Forecaster 2008.* Roanoke, VA: Shandler Enterprises, 2007.

Myers, David G. *Intuition: Its Powers and Perils.* New Haven, CT: Yale University Press, 2002.

Nagel, Rosemarie. "Unraveling in Guessing Games: An Experimental Study." *American Economic Review* 85, no. 5 (1995): 1313–1326.

Nakamoto, Michiyo, and David Wighton. "Citigroup Chief Stays Bullish on Buy-Outs." *The Financial Times,* July 9, 2007.

Newman, M. E. J. "Power Laws, Pareto Distributions and Zipf's Law." *arXiv:cond-mat,* May 29, 2006.

Niesewand, Nonie. "Will Norman Foster and Anthony Caro Cross the Thames in a Blade of Light?" *The Independent,* September 25, 1997.

Nickerson, Raymond S. "Confirmation Bias: A Ubiquitous Phenomenon in Many Guises." *Review of General Psychology* 2, no. 2 (1998): 175–220.

Nisbett, Richard E. *The Geography of Thought: How Asians and Westerners Think Differently ... and Why.* New York: Free Press, 2003.

North, Adrian C., David J. Hargreaves, and Jennifer McKendrick. "In-store Music Affects Product Choice." *Nature* 390 (November 13, 2007): 13.

Nocera, Joe. "On Oil Supply, Opinions Aren't Scarce." *New York Times,* September 10, 2005.

Northcraft, Gregory B., and Margaret A. Neale. "Experts, Amateurs, and Real Estate: An Anchoring-and-Adjustment Perspective on Property Pricing Decisions." *Organizational Behavior and Human Decision Processes* 39, no. 1 (1987): 84–97.

O'Halloran, Ryan. "A 'Foregone Conclusion'?" *Washington Times,* May 30, 2008.

Page, Scott E. "Path Dependence," *Quarterly Journal of Political Science* 1, no. 1 (2006): 87–115.

_____. *The Difference: How the Power of Diversity Creates Better Groups, Firms, Schools, and Societies.* Princeton, NJ: Princeton University Press, 2007.

Paulos, John Allen. *A Mathematician Reads the Newspaper.* New York: Basic Books, 1995.

Pearl, Judea. *Causality: Models, Reasoning, and Inference.* Cambridge: Cambridge University Press, 2000.

Pedulla, Tom. "Big Brown Makes His Run at Immortality." *USA Today*, June 6, 2008.

Perrow, Charles. *Normal Accidents: Living with High-Risk Technologies.* Princeton, NJ: Princeton University Press, 1999.

Pierson, Paul. *Politics in Time: History, Institutions, and Social Analysis.* Princeton, NJ: Princeton University Press, 2004.

Pinker, Steven. *How the Mind Works.* New York: W.W Norton & Company, 1997.

_____. *The Blank Slate: The Modern Denial of Human Nature.* New York: Viking, 2002.

Plassmann, Hilke, John O'Doherty, Baba Shiv, and Antonio Rangel. "Marketing Actions Can Modulate Neural Representations of Experienced Pleasantness." *Proceedings of the National Academy of Sciences* 105, no. 3 (2008): 1050–1054.

Plott, Charles R., and Vernon L. Smith, eds. *Handbook of Experimental Economics Results:* vol. 1. Amsterdam: North-Holland, 2008.

Poundstone, William. *Fortune's Formula: The Untold Story of the Unscientific Betting System That Beat the Casinos and Wall Street.* New York: Hill and Wang, 2005.

Pronovost, Peter. "Testimony before Government Oversight Committee," April 16, 2008.

Rappaport, Alfred, and Michael J. Mauboussin. *Expectations Investing: Reading Stock Prices for Better Returns.* Boston: Harvard Business School Press, 2001.

Reason, James. *Human Error.* Cambridge: Cambridge University Press, 1990.

Redelmeier, Donald A., Paul Rozin, and Daniel Kahneman. "Understanding Patients' Decisions: Cognitive and Emotional Perspectives." *The Journal of the American Medical Association* 270, no. 1 (1993): 72–76.

Roberson, Brian. "The Colonel Blotto Game." *Economic Theory* 29, no. 1 (2006): 1–24.

Roese, Neal J., and James M. Olsen, eds. *What Might Have Been: The Social Psychology of Counterfactual Thinking.* Mahwah, NJ: Lawrence Erlbaum Associates, 1994.

Romer, David. "Do Firms Maximize? Evidence from Professional Football." *The Journal of Political Economy* 114, no. 2 (2006): 340–365.

Rosenbaum, Paul R. *Observational Studies,* 2nd ed. New York: Springer, 2002.

Rosenzweig, Phil. *The Halo Effect ... and the Eight Other Business Delusions That Deceive Managers.* New York: Free Press, 2007.

_____. "The Halo Effect and Other Managerial Delusions." *The McKinsey Quarterly*, no. 1 (February 2007): 77–85.

Ross, Lee. "The Intuitive Psychologist and His Shortcomings." In *Advances in Experimental Social Psychology*, edited by Leonard Berkowitz, 173–220. New York: Academic Press, 1977.

Russell, Bertrand. *The Problems of Philosophy.* Oxford: Oxford University Press, 1959.

Russo, J. Edward, and Paul J. H. Schoemaker. *Winning Decisions: Getting It Right the First Time.* New York: Doubleday, 2002.

Salganik, Matthew J., Peter Sheridan Dodds, and Duncan J. Watts. "Experimental Study of Inequality and Unpredictability in an Artificial Cultural Market." *Science* 311 (February 10, 2006): 854–856.

Salmon, Felix. "Recipe for Disaster: The Formula That Killed Wall Street." *Wired Magazine,* March 2009, 74–79, 112.

Sapolsky, Robert M. *Why Zebras Don't Get Ulcers: An Updated Guide to Stress, Stress-Related Disease, and Coping.* New York: W.H. Freeman and Company, 1994.

Schelling, Thomas C. *Micromotives and Macrobehavior.* New York: W.W. Norton & Company, 1978.

Schultz, Steven. "Freshman Learn About Thinking from Nobel Laureate." *Princeton Weekly Bulletin* 94, no. 3 (2004).

Secrist, Horace. *The Triumph of Mediocrity in Business.* Evanston, IL: Bureau of Business Research, Northwestern University, 1933.

Seeley, Thomas D. *The Wisdom of the Hive.* Cambridge: Harvard University Press, 1995.

Seeley, Thomas D., P. Kirk Visscher, and Kevin M. Passino. "Group Decision Making in Honey Bee Swarms." *American Scientist* 94, no. 3 (2006): 220–229.

Seeley, Thomas D., and P. Kirk Visscher. "Sensory Coding of Nest-site Value in Honeybee Swarms." *The Journal of Experimental Biology* 211, no. 23 (2008): 3691–3697.

Shannon, B., J. Peacock, and M. J. Brown. "Body fatness, television viewing and calorie-intake of a sample of Pennsylvania sixth grade children." *Journal of Nutrition Education* 23, no. 6 (1991): 262–268.

Shapiro, Carl, and Hal Varian. *Information Rules: A Strategic Guide to the Network Economy.* Boston: Harvard Business School Press, 1998.

Shefrin, Hersh. *Behavioral Corporate Finance: Decisions That Create Value.* New York: McGraw-Hill, 2007.

Simon, Herbert A. "The Architecture of Complexity." *Proceedings of the American Philosophical Society* 106, no. 6 (1962): 467–482.

———. *The Sciences of the Artificial,* 3rd ed. Cambridge: MIT Press, 1996.

Simons, Daniel J., and Christopher F. Chabris. "Gorillas in Our Midst: Sustained Inattentional Blindness for Dynamic Events." *Perception* 28, no. 9 (1999): 1059–1074.

Sirower, Mark L. *The Synergy Trap: How Companies Lose the Acquisition Game.* New York: Free Press, 1997.

Slovic, Paul, Melissa Finucane, Ellen Peters, and Donald G. MacGregor. "The Affect Heuristic." In *Heuristics and Biases: The Psychology of Intuitive Judgment,* edited by Thomas Gilovich, Dale Griffin, and Daniel Kahneman, 397–420. Cambridge: Cambridge University Press, 2002.

Smith, Douglas W., and Gary Ferguson. *Decade of the Wolf: Returning the Wild to Yellowstone.* Guilford, CT: The Lyons Press, 2005.

Smith, Vernon L. *Rationality in Economics: Constructivist and Ecological Forms.* Cambridge: Cambridge University Press, 2008.

Sornette, Didier. *Why Stock Markets Crash: Critical Events in Complex Financial Systems.* Princeton, NJ: Princeton University Press, 2003.

Stanovich, Keith E. *What Intelligence Tests Miss: The Psychology of Rational Thought*. New Haven, CT: Yale University Press, 2009.

Stecklow, Steve, and Diya Gullapalli. "A Money-Fund Manager's Fateful Shift." *Wall Street Journal*, December 8, 2008.

Steinwald, A. Bruce. "Primary Care Professionals: Recent Supply Trends, Projections, and Valuation of Services." *Testimony Before the Committee on Health Education, Labor, and Pensions, U.S. Senate*, February 12, 2008.

Sterman, John D. *Business Dynamics: Systems Thinking and Modeling for a Complex World*. Boston: Irwin McGraw-Hill, 2000.

Sterman, John D., and Linda Booth Sweeney. "Managing Complex Dynamic Systems: Challenge and Opportunity for Naturalistic Decision-Making Theory." In *How Professionals Make Decisions*, edited by Henry Montgomery, Raanan Lipshitz, and Berndt Brehmer, 57–90. Mahway, NJ: Lawrence Erlbaum Associates, 2005.

Stigler, Stephen M. *The History of Statistics: The Measurement of Uncertainty before 1990*. Cambridge: Harvard University Press, 1986.

_____. *Statistics on the Table: The History of Statistical Concepts and Methods*. Cambridge: Harvard University Press, 1999.

_____. "Milton Friedman and Statistics." In *The Collected Writings of Milton Friedman*, edited by Robert Leeson. New York: Routledge, forthcoming.

Strogatz, Steven. *Sync: The Emerging Science of Spontaneous Order*. New York: Hyperion, 2003.

Strogatz, Steven H., Daniel M. Abrams, Allan McRobie, Bruno Eckhardt, and Edward Ott. "Crowd Synchrony on the Millennium Bridge." *Nature* 483 (November 3, 2005): 43–44.

Sudjic, Deyan. *Blade of Light: The Story of London's Millennium Bridge*. London: Penguin Books, 2001.

Sulloway, Frank J. *Born to Rebel: Birth Order, Family Dynamics, and Creative Lives*. New York: Pantheon, 1996.

Sunder, Shyam. "Relationship Between Accounting Changes and Stock Prices: Problems of Measurement and Some Empirical Evidence." *Journal of Accounting Research: Empirical Research in Accounting: Selected Studies 1973* 11 (1973): 1–45.

Sunstein, Cass R. *Why Societies Need Dissent*. Cambridge: Harvard University Press, 2003.

_____. *Infotopia: How Many Minds Produce Knowledge*. Oxford: Oxford University Press, 2006.

Surowiecki, James *The Wisdom of Crowds: Why the Many Are Smarter Than the Few and How Collective Wisdom Shapes Business, Economies, Societies, and Nations*. New York: Doubleday and Company, 2004.

_____. "Did Lehman Brothers' Failure Matter?" *The New Yorker.com*, March 9, 2009.

Taleb, Nassim Nicholas. *Fooled by Randomness: The Hidden Role of Chance in Life and in the Markets*, 2nd ed. New York: Thomson Texere, 2004.

_____ . *The Black Swan: The Impact of the Highly Improbable*. New York: Random House, 2007.

Tavris, Carol, and Elliot Aronson, *Mistakes Were Made (but not by* me*): Why We Justify Foolish Beliefs, Bad Decisions, and Hurtful Acts* Orlando, FL: Harcourt, Inc., 2007.

Taylor, Shelley E., and Jonathan D. Brown. "Illusion and Well-Being: A Social Psychological Perspective on Mental Health." *Psychological Bulletin* 103, no. 2 (1988): 193–210.

Tetlock, Philip E. *Expert Political Judgment: How Good Is It? How Can We Know?* Princeton, NJ: Princeton University Press, 2005.

Thaler, Richard H. "Anomalies: The Winner's Curse." *The Journal of Economic Perspectives* 2, no. 1 (1988): 191–202.

_____. "Anomalies: The Ultimatum Game." *The Journal of Economic Perspectives* 2, no. 4 (1988): 195–206.

_____. "From Homo Economicus to Homo Sapiens." *The Journal of Economic Perspectives* 14, no. 1 (2000): 133–141.

Thaler, Richard H., and Cass R. Sunstein. *Nudge: Improving Decisions About Health, Wealth, and Happiness.* New Haven, CT: Yale University Press, 2008.

Thompson, Clive. "If You Liked This, You're Sure to Love That." *New York Times Magazine*, November 23, 2008.

Thorndike, Edward L. "A Constant Error in Psychological Ratings." *Journal of Applied Psychology* 4, no. 1 (1920): 469–477.

Thorp, Edward O. *The Mathematics of Gambling.* Hollywood, CA: Gambling Times, 1984.

Tilson, Whitney, and Glenn Tongue, *More Mortgage Meltdown: 6 Ways to Profit in These Bad Times.* New York: John Wiley & Sons, 2009.

Tomlinson, Richard, and Paola Hjelt, "Dethroning Percy Barnevik," *Fortune International*, April 1, 2002, 38–41.

Townsend, Frederic. "Birth Order and Rebelliousness: Reconstructing the Research in *Born to Rebel.*" *Politics and the Life Sciences* 19, no. 2 (2000): 135–156.

Treynor, Jack L. "Market Efficiency and the Bean Jar Experiment." *Financial Analysts Journal*, May–June 1987, 50–53.

Turner, Mark. *The Literary Mind.* New York: Oxford University Press, 1996.

Tversky, Amos, and Daniel Kahneman. "Belief in the Law of Small Numbers." *Psychological Bulletin* 76, no. 2 (1971): 105–110.

_____. "Judgment under Uncertainty: Heuristics and Biases" *Science* 185, no. 4157 (1974): 1124–1131.

Tyszka, Tadeusz, and Piotr Zielonka. "Expert Judgments: Financial Analysts Versus Weather Forecasters." *The Journal of Psychology and Financial Markets* 3, no. 3 (2002): 152–160.

Vedantam, Shankar. "Vote Your Conscience. If You Can." *Washington Post*, December 31, 2007, A3.

Waitzkin, Josh. *The Art of Learning: A Journey in the Pursuit of Excellence.* New York: Free Press, 2007.

Wallace, James. "Boeing Executive Faults Some 787 Suppliers." *Seattle Post-Intelligencer*, November 1, 2007.

Watts, Duncan J. "A Simple Model of Global Cascades on Random Networks." *Proceedings of the National Academy of Sciences* 99, no. 9, April 30, 2002: 5766–5771.

_____. *Six Degrees: The Science of a Connect Age.* New York: W.W. Norton & Company, 2003.

_____. "Is Justin Timberlake a Product of Cumulative Advantage?" *New York Times Magazine*, April 15, 2007.

Weinstein, Neil D. "Unrealistic Optimism about Future Life Events." *Journal of Personality and Social Psychology* 39, no. 5 (1980): 806–820.

West, Geoffrey B., and James H. Brown. "Life's Universal Scaling Laws." *Physics Today,* September 2004, 36–42.

Westen, Drew, Pavel S. Blagov, Keith Harenski, Clint Kilts, and Stephan Hamann. "Neural Bases of Motivated Reasoning: An fMRI Study of Emotional Constraints on Partisan Political Judgment in the 2004 U.S. Presidential Election." *Journal of Cognitive Neuroscience* 18, no. 11 (2006): 1947–1958.

Westen, Drew. *The Political Brain: The Role of Emotion in Deciding the Fate of the Nation.* New York: Public Affairs, 2007.

Wiseman, Richard. *Did You Spot the Gorilla? How to Recognize Hidden Opportunities.* London: Random House, 2004.

Wolff, Alexander. "SI Flashback: That Old Black Magic." *Sports Illustrated,* January 21, 2002.

Wolpert, Lewis. *Six Impossible Things Before Breakfast: The Evolutionary Origins of Belief.* New York: W.W. Norton, 2007.

Yariv, Leeat. "I'll See It When I Believe It—A Simple Model of Cognitive Consistency." Discussion paper no. 1352, Cowles Foundation, February 2002.

Zajonc, R. B., ed. *The Selected Works of R. B. Zajonc.* New York: John Wiley & Sons, 2004.

Zimbardo, Philip. *The Lucifer Effect: Understanding How Good People Turn Evil.* New York: Random House, 2007.

Zweig, Jason. "Do You Sabotage Yourself? Daniel Kahneman Has Done More Than Anyone Else to Explain Why Most of Us Make So Many Mistakes as Investors—And What We Can Do About It." *Money,* May 1, 2001.

_____. "Peter Bernstein Interview: He May Know More About Investing than Anyone Alive." *Money,* October 15, 2004, 143–148.

_____. *Your Money and Your Brain: How the New Science of Neuroeconomics Can Help Make You Rich.* New York: Simon & Schuster, 2007.

Note: An *n* following a page number denotes a reference in a source note.

Michael J. Mauboussin is Chief Investment Strategist at Legg Mason Capital Management. Prior to joining LMCM, he served as managing director and chief U.S. investment strategist at Credit Suisse.

Mauboussin's work focuses on the investment process from both the company's and the investor's standpoint. His multidisciplinary approach draws from fields including finance, competitive strategy, psychology, and complex systems theory. Mauboussin's ideas have been featured in national publications including the *Wall Street Journal, Fortune, Forbes*, and *SmartMoney*.

He is the author of *More Than You Know: Finding Financial Wisdom in Unconventional Places* (Columbia University Press, 2006) and coauthor, with Alfred Rappaport, of *Expectations Investing: Reading Stock Prices for Better Returns* (Harvard Business School Press, 2001). *More Than You Know* was named as one of "The 100 Best Business Books of All Time" by 1-800-CEO-READ. Mauboussin has also authored or coauthored articles for the *Harvard Business Review, Journal of Applied Corporate Finance, Financial Management, Time*, and *Fortune*.

Mauboussin has been an Adjunct Professor of Finance at Columbia Business School since 1993 and is on the faculty of the Heilbrunn Center for Graham and Dodd Investing. In 2009, he received the Dean's Award for Teaching Excellence by an Adjunct Faculty Member. Mauboussin is also affiliated with the Santa Fe Institute, the founding institution of complexity science and a global leader in multidisciplinary research.

Mauboussin received an AB in government from Georgetown University. He lives in Darien, Connecticut, with his wife and five children.